T0248175

PRAISE FOR *DO GOOD WHILE DOING WELL*

"*Do Good While Doing Well* is what you and I have been waiting for: a step-by-step guide to investing in the change that matters most to you. If you're looking to ignite your passion and purpose, this book is your firestarter."

Mel Robbins, *New York Times* bestselling author and host of
The Mel Robbins Podcast

"With *Do Good While Doing Well*, Marcia has done a tremendous service to both seasoned investors and those new to the field. She demystifies angel investing and shows it as a viable tool for societal change, providing readers with the knowledge and confidence to take action. It's a compelling read that will undoubtedly inspire many to invest with intention."

Dr. Marshall Goldsmith, Thinkers50 #1 executive coach and *New York Times*
bestselling author of *The Earned Life, Triggers,* and
What Got You Here Won't Get You There

"*Do Good While Doing Well* is a beacon of clarity for anyone who's ever felt overwhelmed by the world of early-stage investing. It demystifies the process, showing us that making a difference is within reach for everyone, creating a legacy of change."

Josh Linkner, five-time tech entrepreneur, *New York Times* bestselling author,
and venture capitalist

"This book is a must-read for aspiring changemakers, from founders to funders and every consumer in between. By breaking down barriers and inspiring action that builds legacy and impact, Marcia helps you find your best pathways that live up to the promise to 'do good while doing well.' By the end of this insightful read, you'll be raising two hands to be part of the village of change—the incredible entrepreneurs building a brighter future for us all!"

Nicola Corzine, CEO, Nasdaq Entrepreneurial Center

"An inspiring and insightful guide that challenges and changes the way we think about investments, this book is a powerful tool for anyone wanting to leverage their financial resources for social good."

Dorie Clark, *Wall Street Journal* bestselling author of *The Long Game*; and executive education faculty, Columbia Business School

"Marcia's years of investment experience and her passionate journey to change the world make this a must-read for everyone who wishes they could do more to influence outcomes. Learn how to 'be the change you want to see in the world' while hearing interesting stories about the trailblazers and innovators who are carving their own paths and shaping the future in unique and inspiring ways."

Patrick Gouhin, CEO, Angel Capital Association

"*Do Good While Doing Well* is a must-read for anyone who cares about bridging the gender gap in venture capital. It's a compelling narrative that not only sheds light on the challenges women face in securing VC funding, but also offers actionable insights for making impactful investments. A must-read for changemakers."

Catherine Gray, CEO, She Angel Investors; executive producer, *Show Her the Money*; and host, *Invest In Her* podcast

"In *Do Good While Doing Well*, the complex world of early-stage investing is unraveled with clarity and passion. It's a compelling call to action for anyone looking to be a part of meaningful change, providing a roadmap to invest with purpose and profit."

Catherine Mott, founder/managing partner, BTVC Fund, BlueTree Capital Group

"*Do Good While Doing Well* serves as a source of inspiration for a new generation of investors. This book proves you can align your investments with your values, supporting diversity and driving change while reaping the rewards."

Pocket Sun, cofounder and managing partner of SoGal Ventures

"Marcia's passion for introducing others to the various options of early-stage investing jumps from the pages of *Do Good While Doing Well*. Page by page, she reveals details of what used to be a little-known secret of the wealthy. This is a must-read for anyone new to the early-stage entrepreneurship and innovation ecosystem!"

Nicole Washington, Angel Capital Association board member,
Ohio Tech Angels

"If you aspire to accelerate positive change, *Do Good While Doing Well* will open your eyes to powerful new pathways to make a meaningful difference. By collectively investing our time, talent, and treasure, we can empower more purpose-driven founders to overcome barriers to success. Under Marcia's mentorship, I've benefited from her practical and inspiring guidance. Now you can too!"

Sue Bevan Baggott, former global innovation leader at Procter & Gamble,
founder of Power Within Consulting, angel investor,
and startup advisor

"*Do Good While Doing Well* stands as an essential manifesto for anyone looking to invest with intention and heart. If you care about economic equity and mobility, then you want to make an investment in this book. Discover how your financial actions can paint a brighter future for the world—Marcia's visionary work is your first step."

Angel Gambino, founder of Angel Club

www.amplifypublishinggroup.com

Do Good While Doing Well: Invest for Change, Reap Financial Rewards, and Increase Your Happiness

For more information, please contact:
Amplify Publishing, an imprint of Amplify Publishing Group
620 Herndon Parkway, Suite 220
Herndon, VA 20170
info@amplifypublishing.com

Library of Congress Control Number: 2023923138

CPSIA Code: PRV0424A

ISBN-13: 979-8-89138-124-7

Printed in the United States

For my Mama:
From heaven, I know you are inspiring entrepreneurs every day to find a cure for ALS.

Invest for Change, Reap Financial Rewards,
and Increase Your Happiness

DO
GOOD
while
DOING
WELL

MARCIA DAWOOD

amplify
an imprint of Amplify Publishing Group

TABLE OF CONTENTS

INTRODUCTION

WHEN I STEP OFF THE ICONIC TED RED DOT and into the audience, a line of people waits for me. I've just given my talk about investing for change, *Do Good While Doing Well*, at TEDx Charlotte. As I meet the people standing in line, each asks the same question: "What do I do next?"

The answer to that question can be different for everyone. The things we are passionate about are different for all of us, and the amount of time or money we can devote not only differs by person but also based on what is going on in our lives. But there is one undeniable commonality: we want to make a difference.

I never thought that as one person, I would be able to effect the change I want to see in the world. I thought that was for big companies and charities to work on. Not me. My career started in corporate America, working for the same company for more than sixteen years. And then, one day, I accepted an invitation to a meeting to see a few entrepreneurs talk about their companies. I was fascinated. People were out there working on innovation near me? And they were interested in *my* help? How could I help entrepreneurs grow their businesses? What did I even know about entrepreneurship? And I didn't have the kind of money the people you see on shows like *Shark Tank* do, so how could it be for me? These and so many other questions went through my head when I first learned about angel investing in 2012.

Through angel investing, I was able to find and engage with companies working on interesting innovations that I cared about, things that could make a real difference in the world. I've met many different types of people I would have never interacted with otherwise. And I found a way to use my time and my dollars for change.

You, too, may be wondering how you can make a difference. We hear stories about groups of people coming together, and due to their collective efforts, big things happen. Take the Ice Bucket Challenge back in 2014. A small group started this to raise money for the ALS Association. ALS is not very common, but it is a ruthless disease that unfortunately took my mom's life in 2018. The challenge went viral and raised more money and awareness in support of ALS than the association had ever seen in its history. But can individuals make a difference too? The answer is yes! You will hear stories throughout this book about start-up companies that wouldn't have made it if they hadn't gotten help early on from just one or a few people. People like you and me!

The key factor that elevates a small business to an investable startup is its foundation for rapid growth and scalability. Many people I have spoken to over the years believe working with start-ups, especially investing in them, is meant only for the rich and well-connected. This is simply not true. My mission to demystify this thinking began on my podcast, *The Angel Next Door*, and now here in this book. You will discover why charity alone cannot solve the world's problems, and we can be the change we want to see in the world by *investing* in change.

Like the audience members at my TEDx talk, you may be wondering how. How can individuals make a real difference? Well, in 2016, the Securities and Exchange Commission, where I now sit on an advisory committee, changed the rules, so now just about anyone can invest in a start-up for as little as $50. Much more on this throughout the book.

As of 2024, according to the Angel Capital Association (ACA), there are only about three hundred thousand angel investors in the US. That is less than a fraction of 1 percent of the US population! We need more people to participate in supporting start-ups so that we can see change happen faster. And not just innovative changes in areas like health care and climate change. We also need to see changes in how much funding goes to underrepresented entrepreneurs—this includes women and people of color. According to Bloomberg, women receive less than 3 percent of venture capital funding, and people of color get much less than that.[1] These disparities have persisted for many years.

To change the amount of funding going to innovative companies, especially ones led by underrepresented founders, we must increase the number and diversity of people making these early-stage investment decisions. To do that, we need more people to become aware of their opportunities to participate in creating change at all levels.

Additionally, we need to reframe our thinking around investing. Many people hear the word *investing* and think that to invest they need to focus only on evaluating the potential financial gain. There's a common worry about feeling judged by others or doubting ourselves if investment choices don't yield anticipated outcomes. This mindset needs a refresh. Years ago, a returns-only focus might have had merit, but now there is more to it. Our investments can have an impact beyond financial returns. We can make choices to *do good while doing well.*

Donating to charity isn't the only way to do good, and traditional investing isn't the only way to do well. We can drive positive, impactful change, feel good about the entrepreneurs we are backing, and still seek financial returns.

Innovative start-ups are tackling major issues, like treatments for diseases or reducing poverty. Yet all too frequently, their groundbreaking ideas were abandoned, metaphorically left on the cutting-room floor, due to insufficient funding needed to turn these ambitious concepts into reality. Imagine the sense of happiness and pride you would feel if you were part of advancing such transformative ventures, directly contributing to bringing life-changing ideas to fruition.

Your journey to make a difference, reap financial rewards, and increase your happiness begins here.

Chapter One

PUT YOUR MONEY
WHERE YOUR HEART IS

I WANTED TO MAKE A DIFFERENCE IN THE WORLD as far back as I can remember. In the home of my mom's best friend with her towering stacks of Avon catalogs, my desire to make a mark found its first expression. I was fourteen years old, and my mom and I were visiting Becky, also the local Avon lady. I used to love looking through the newest books featuring cosmetics and fragrances. I especially liked the lip gloss at that age. I was in the other room playing with the dog, Charlie, when I overheard my mom say, "Do you want Marcia to help you?"

I was summoned, and as I made my way to the living room, my mind raced with ideas of what tasks I could be asked to help with. My parents had just started giving me an allowance for doing chores around the house, which helped me realize I was money motivated, but I was still a teenager who would rather lie around watching TV.

When I entered the room, I'm sure I had one of those confused yet disgusted adolescent looks on my face. Becky and Mom looked at me, then at the stack of books, and then back at me.

Becky, who was very direct, blurted, "How would you like to earn some extra money with me?"

"What do I have to do?" I asked.

"I need someone to deliver Avon books around the different neighborhoods where my customers live."

The money-motivated side of me was excited, but the lazy side spoke first. "That seems like a lot of walking." Becky and my mom both burst out laughing, leaving me feeling a little embarrassed. "What did I say?"

"In the car," Becky said, still laughing. "I'll drive you around in the car, and you will go to each door and drop off the books."

I envisioned myself having to go to every house in the neighborhood, which seemed daunting. Then Becky explained, "We'll go to about fifty total houses. It'll take about three hours, and we'll do it every two weeks. I'll pay you fifteen dollars each time you help me."

As I considered my first offer of employment, I thought, *Fifteen dollars is a lot of money; that would be thirty dollars a month.* My self-absorbed teenage thoughts continued. Becky stood up and walked toward the kitchen. She was limping.

I whispered to my mom, "Why is Becky limping?"

"She has MS."

"What is MS?"

"Multiple sclerosis. It's a disease where her immune system starts to attack healthy cells. It makes it harder for her to get around. That's why she's asking for your help."

Delivering Avon books became my first job. Becky and I had fun driving around the neighborhoods as we sang along to the Top 40 hits on the radio.

Sadly, I watched her gait change over the years until she could no longer walk. I wondered, *Why can't someone do anything about this?* I wanted so much to help Becky get better, but I had no idea how.

On the night of my high school graduation, the anticipation of adulthood was thick in the air, punctuated by the smiles and tears of proud parents. Among them was my father, who, as we gathered for the family celebration afterward, handed me a small, gift-wrapped box adorned with a perfect red bow. The mysterious box had a certain heft to it, and my mind raced with possibilities of what could be inside. My best friend had just gotten a new watch for her birthday. Could they have heard me admiring it? Or maybe something more personal, a keepsake handed down through generations?

With my parents' eyes on me, I carefully unwrapped the package, savoring the moment of discovery. Inside, I found something unexpected yet very meaningful—a stone magnet etched with the words "Be the change you want to see in the world." The quote, attributed to Mahatma Gandhi, resonated with me immediately.

A surge of empowerment washed over me, a sensation that seemed to resonate with the core of who I was and who I wanted to become. I felt fearless, invincible, ready to conquer the world. My heart pounded in agreement as I mentally shouted, *YES! I want to be the change.*

But as the excitement settled, a more complex question began to take shape, tugging at the corners of my newfound confidence. *How do I do that? How can I, a single individual, fresh out of high school, make a real difference and effect change in the world that lies before me?*

That night, my father didn't just give me a gift. He put me on a mission. A mission that would take me down roads I never expected, filled with trials, triumphs, and the relentless pursuit of a goal that once seemed unattainable. A mission to be the change, to make a difference, one step at a time.

At the tender age of eighteen, I wasn't sure where to start. Do I dive into the world of volunteering, or perhaps channel my energy into raising funds for a deserving cause? You, like me, may want to do big things, but how do we know we are making a meaningful difference and genuinely moving the needle? Does my twenty-five-dollar donation to the American Cancer Society get us closer to curing cancer? Maybe it does, but if that's the case, then how?

As I wondered, *How can one person make a difference?*, I would also hear people say things like, "Everyone's contributions matter." I found this all very confusing.

I started to get a taste of making a difference while I was on my *magical* college internship at Walt Disney World, Florida. A friend told me about an annual 150-mile bike ride supporting MS. Wow, an event to raise money to research better treatments or a cure for MS! Finally, I had found something I could do to help Becky.

The ride was such a great experience. I was biking through Florida. It was sunny and flat. And I thought, *I want to do this event every year. I'm doing good raising money for a cause I care about and having fun too.* So I did it again the following year, except now I was back in Pittsburgh, Pennsylvania. Pittsburgh is *not* sunny and definitely not flat. It is very hilly.

At the end of the first day, after eighty miles were behind me, I rounded a corner. I saw the finish line, but there was a huge hill I still had to climb. I made it, but that night I had to get ice from the cafeteria to put on my thighs. They were on fire!

The next morning, for the first five miles or so, my thighs were screaming, but then, miraculously, the last sixty-five miles were much flatter. I finished the ride, which ended overlooking Lake Erie with some beautiful views. I did this ride year after year, and I became one of the top fundraisers. I was really proud. I found a way to *do good* by investing my time and "thigh power" to make a positive impact. And I found a way to help a cause I care about. Every year I would write Becky's name on the back of my jersey so everyone could see who I was riding for.

Throughout my adult life, I believed I was doing "the best I could" to give back by volunteering or donating to charity or helping with fundraising efforts. However, I had no idea what the money was really being used for. Plus, I didn't know if the amount was "good" or "not making any difference at all" because my contribution was so small. I needed a benchmark. I was looking for how I could make an impact in the world that was aligned with the changes I wanted to see that was measurable and verifiable.

In 2020, Americans donated $471 billion to charities. A record year, thanks to COVID, and that's *a lot* of money. Maybe you contributed as one of the donors. If so, do you know what your money was used for? Did you feel like you made a difference? I was shocked when I learned $471 billion represents only about 1 percent of the value of all the companies publicly traded on the US stock market. If we want to effect significant change, we need to look not just to nonprofits and place the burden on them, but also look at innovative for-profit companies too. Invest when they are small, and help them grow.

Charity alone will not fix the world's problems. To *be the change*, we must also *invest* in the change we want to see in the world.

In my search for answers, I would eventually discover a powerful way to transform my dollars into making a real, measurable difference—an avenue to drive change that opened a whole world of possibilities and opportunities.

A WAY TO USE MY DOLLARS DIFFERENTLY

After college and through the early 2000s, I spent my time working in corporate America. I was doing what I could to get ahead and help others advance in the workplace, and each year I would make some donations to my charities of choice. It wasn't until 2012 when my husband, Izzy, and I were living in Pittsburgh that I discovered a way to use my time and dollars differently. It was January 2012 when Izzy came home from work and told me we were invited to an "angel investing" meeting. I had never heard this term before, so I asked him to explain.

Izzy, who works in finance, said, "Now that we are getting past the 2008/2009 financial crisis, people were looking for ways to invest in 'alternative assets.'"

"What's an alternative asset?" I asked.

"Things like art, collectibles, and real estate," he explained. "Alternative assets are increasingly appealing to investors seeking diversification beyond traditional options like stocks or mutual funds. This attractiveness stems from their lack of correlation with the conventional market. For instance, the value of a piece of art hinges on the dynamics of supply and demand within the art market, as well as the artist's popularity, rather than being influenced by corporate earnings or economic updates. Additionally, holding a diverse array of asset types ensures a more balanced portfolio. This diversification strategy reduces the risk of financial loss, as it avoids the pitfall of concentrating all investments in a single area, or putting all your eggs in one basket."

I didn't follow the stock market prior to 2008. At that time, I had a small 401(k) plan with my employer that had been slowly growing over the years. I read in the news the stock market was dropping and people were panic-selling, as I heard it called. I remember getting a statement in the mail showing the balance of my 401(k) plan. I was amazed at how much less the balance was than just a few months prior. I quickly learned about market volatility. In contrast to the unpredictable fluctuations of public markets, my neighbor bought his wife a piece of jewelry for $4,000 in 2008. Fifteen years later, its value had multiplied tenfold. Slow and steady increases in value can be very attractive to investors, especially those who do not have the time or desire to be watching their assets closely. An *angel investment* is a form of an alternative asset. Simply put, angel investing is when someone invests their own money into a private company, usually an early-stage company, or what is better known as a start-up.

In the beginning, I was feeling a little overwhelmed by the idea of searching for different things to invest in. I hadn't thought much about this topic before. I'd been working in corporate

America for many years in sales, marketing, and operations—not finance. I wondered, *Do I even know enough to go to this meeting?*

But in those early meetings, as I listened to entrepreneurs talk about all the innovation out there, I was completely hooked. I had no idea so much was happening right in my own backyard, not to mention the rest of the country. I felt like I'd been living under a rock, and now I was realizing the world has so many bright, beautiful flowers. I learned about a company working on speech-to-text hardware that could interpret the speakers' feelings. Whoa. I saw a company making a peat moss substitute out of recycled newspaper, allowing plant growers to use less water.

I started going to angel investing group meetings regularly, first in Pittsburgh and then in the four other cities we lived in over the next ten years. At first it seemed cumbersome to learn about a new group in a new town, but I quickly learned every angel group, while similar, operates a little differently. It gets to evaluate different companies, and every start-up has its own unique flair. I was learning so much just by watching other angels. Not to mention I was making new friends, people I wouldn't normally have met from working in the education industry for over sixteen years. Angels come from all backgrounds—yet another reason I wanted to become more involved.

One of the companies I saw early on, Cognition Therapeutics, was working on a drug to slow down and even reverse Alzheimer's disease. Little did I know, when I first saw this company, how much I would be learning over the next several years about neurological diseases.

WHEN MY WHY GOT MUCH STRONGER

On the afternoon of January 27, 2016, I got a phone call that changed my life. You know how people talk about pre-something and post-something like pre-COVID and post-COVID? For me, there is pre–January 2016 and post. When the call came, I was in the airport traveling to my new home in Dallas, Texas. What a change. I'd lived in the Northeast my whole life, mostly in Pennsylvania. Little did I know how much change was about to happen in my life as I answered the phone.

Several months prior to this phone call, during a visit with my parents, my mom and I went for a walk. We did this often; it was my parents' main form of exercise. As we were headed up a hill, I noticed she wasn't moving as quickly as she usually did, and she casually mentioned something about her right leg. I chalked it up to aging, not thinking much of it. Within a few weeks, the "something" in her right leg wasn't going away; she was limping. She made an appointment to see a doctor. Between the summer of 2015 and January 2016, she saw multiple doctors of multiple specialties. None of them had answers. One offered to perform surgery on her back. When we asked why he thought this was necessary and what the outcome would be, he had no idea. He simply thought it was "worth a try."

After searching for months to find a doctor with some answers, my parents had an appointment to see a neuromuscular neurosurgeon on the morning of January 27, 2016. We were hopeful that if we could just figure out what was going on, we could fix it.

After the appointment, the phone call came from my dad. I could barely understand him through his tears, and my mom was sobbing in the background. My mind was racing, trying to think of what they could possibly have been told. Whatever it was, at that moment, before I heard the diagnosis, I was optimistic we could come up with a treatment plan to get her healthy again. But the next moment changed everything. The reality was much worse than I could have imagined: amyotrophic lateral sclerosis (ALS), also known as Lou Gehrig's Disease.

I'd heard of ALS, but I didn't really understand what it meant. Dr. Google helped me understand over the next hour or so. ALS is a neurological disorder that prevents the brain from telling the body to move its muscles. It starts with being unable to walk or talk and eventually being unable to breathe. Less than a fraction of one percent of the US population is affected by ALS. We hear more about its sister diseases, Parkinson's, and Alzheimer's. All three are neurodegenerative disorders characterized by advancing deterioration of the nervous system. Each disease, and the severity of the disease, affects the human body differently, but they are all related.

We were devastated and desperate for answers. So little is known about the causes, and the treatments are effective in only a small percentage of patients. We went looking for help. The ALS Association was generous in providing the items needed as her disease progressed and her mobility decreased: walkers, wheelchairs, and stairlifts, as well as support groups. But they couldn't help with a treatment or a cure. This was the first time in my life that my family was *receiving* from a charity. I was used to being on the giving side. A few years prior, I participated in the Ice Bucket Challenge, having no idea how closely this disease would touch my life. That challenge raised a significant amount of money for the ALS Association as well as awareness of the disease. But all the money in the world wasn't going to get us the cure we needed right now. I remember thinking, *Why didn't I pay more attention to the information about ALS at the time of the challenge?* As if I could have helped come up with a cure if I had started then. I felt so helpless. I wanted to do something to make a difference. First to cure my mom now, but also to ensure her fate would not be mine.

HOW IT FEELS BEING AN INVESTOR WHERE YOU WANT TO SEE CHANGE

I didn't become an investor in Cognition Therapeutics (CogRx) when I first learned about them in 2012. I watched their progress for some time, a tip I'll share more about later. However, I must have had some kind of fortuitous intuition that this company would be significant to me because I did invest in 2015, prior to my mom's diagnosis. In 2016, as soon as I figured out that Alzheimer's, the primary disease CogRx was working on, and ALS were related diseases, I could not call my friend and CEO of the company Hank Safferstein fast enough. CogRx was working on a new pathway to deliver medication to the brain. If successful, not just Alzheimer's but also other related neurological diseases would face a formidable adversary keeping them at bay. I thought, *Could I already be an investor in a company working on a cure for these horrible diseases? Could this save my mom?*

Unfortunately, not in time. CogRx is making significant progress, but they were not fast enough to save my mom, who, sadly, passed away in 2018. Innovative health-care companies, especially ones making pharmaceuticals, take a lot of time and a lot of money. I vividly remember the day I wrote the check to invest in CogRx. I thought, *Even if I lose this money, if progress is made toward ending Alzheimer's disease, I will feel great knowing I was a part of it.*

I was also excited to support a female entrepreneur. Hank was the CEO, but the science behind the company was the work of Dr. Susan Catalano. I was appalled when I learned that women get less than 3 percent of the funding going to early-stage companies. Three percent? Women are roughly 50 percent of the US population; I can't believe they only have 3 percent of the good ideas. More on this in Chapter 5. Yet another reason I wanted to be a part of this change.

According to the Annual Report in 2022 of the US Securities and Exchange Commission (SEC), Office of the Advocate for Small Business Capital Formation, $29.1 billion was invested by angels in 69,060 entrepreneurial ventures.[2] Technology and health care were high on the list of the companies getting funded. All of this was on the rise from the previous year. New York and California, the states that historically have gotten a large percent, were not the only ones where funding was received. Innovation is happening all over the US, as well as all over the world. While $29.1 billion is a lot of money, it's a drop in the bucket to what is needed to really impact change. Just a few paragraphs ago, I mentioned that $471 billion is small compared to the US stock market. We can do more. You can be a part of it.

ANYBODY CAN INVEST IN CHANGE

Before we go any further, let's address the elephant or elephants in the room. The top questions I get about angel investing are:

"Isn't this only for rich people?"

"How do I even know about or get access to this?"

"Isn't this very risky?"

"Is there a way to participate without money?"

As far as being only for the rich, for the most part, that used to be true. But three significant changes have occurred since 2016 which makes early-stage investing much more accessible. We will dive into more detail throughout this book.

1. The SEC changed the rules, and now anyone can invest in a private company for as little as $50 through equity crowdfunding.

2. Philanthropic dollars (money used to donate to charity) can be used to invest in a start-up and still get a tax write-off by using a donor-advised fund (DAF).

3. Revenue-based financing (RBF) allows the investor to lend money to a start-up and be paid back each month by the company, sharing a percent of the revenue with the investor until the loan is paid off.

Access. Getting access used to be for the people who lived in Silicon Valley or knew the "right people." You had to be invited to invest. Golf course conversations could lead to investment opportunities. That is simply not the case anymore. Using the three ways listed above, you can get access to start-ups and innovation without a lot of money or an invitation. Also, the COVID pandemic forced so many angel activities to move online, which broadened their reach. Before the pandemic, becoming a member of an angel group, like Queen City Angels in Cincinnati, Ohio, was unheard of if you didn't live in the area. Now, many angel groups take members from all over the country and hold most meetings in a hybrid style if not completely online.

Risk. We have a saying in angel world, and I'm not sure who came up with it. The saying goes: "Out of ten companies, five will fail, three will return the money invested, one will return the investment with a small return, and one may hit with a larger return." So how do you decide which ten to invest in? You will learn more about that throughout the book, and you don't need to always make the decisions, at least not alone. Risk is mitigated with diversification, and I will cover how to diversify and minimize risk. The more companies an investor gets exposure to, the lower the risk becomes that all money will be lost. Until recently, angels mainly invested directly into one company at a time. But investing in an angel fund allows someone to make one investment, and that fund invests in multiple companies, much like a mutual fund works in the public markets. And what about the companies that don't make it? The start-up world is a learning experience. The most successful founders have had failures in their past. I try not to think about the companies that don't make it as failures but more as the learnings for everyone involved that will make the next innovation or company likelier to succeed.

I've made many mistakes investing in early-stage companies.

They are all risky, and there is always a reason to say no. But as you look closer into the founders and their innovations, you can find your yes. How will you know which companies to pick? I'll cover that, and the good news is that after 2015, many options opened up for investing in start-up companies.

Non-Financial Investment. I quickly learned that yes, start-up companies need money, but they need a lot more than just money. Entrepreneurs are usually very good at their craft, but often they aren't so good at the business part. So being an angel can mean investing money, or time and expertise, or all of the above. You don't need to have a PhD or be an intellectual property attorney to offer a company your expertise. You could be someone with bookkeeping experience, or you may have worked in human resources. These skills are extremely valuable to a start-up. Building a company is hard work, which also takes a village. More on this later.

I had no idea this start-up world existed at the beginning of 2012. But since then, I have learned about hundreds of exciting products and technologies and gotten more comfortable with angel financial terms. I've met many people across a variety of industries I would have never met otherwise and now have an arsenal of interesting cocktail-party stories. Not to mention, dinner-table conversation with Izzy and my three stepsons is never dull!

There are a variety of ways investing in change can be doable for you. Some may take more time, some may take more money, and some, once set up, may take very little of either. I found out angel investing existed because I was invited to a group meeting. And I was fortunate enough to have some extra income (and time) each year, which I used to invest so I could learn by doing. But I don't recommend taking this approach. When I started, very few accessible angel funds existed, equity crowdfunding had not been approved, and revenue-based financing was barely talked about. I wish I'd had a guide to navigate this fascinating yet often untalked-about way to make change in the world. *Do Good While Doing Well* is your guide. And you don't have to be perfect; you just need to try. I will lay a path for you to more effectively drive the change you want to see in the world that can bring you both emotional and financial rewards.

If you are thinking, *I don't have much or any time or money, but I do care about contributing to change*, this book is still for you. Increasing your awareness of the types of innovation happening in your town, your state, and even the country can make a difference. We all make decisions regularly about where we shop, where we bank, and which restaurants we choose. While most of those businesses are not scalable start-ups, meaning not all have the potential to grow into large companies, the founders are all entrepreneurs.

Consciously deciding to support businesses owned by those who are underrepresented can make a big difference, especially in a local community. Underrepresented includes gender, race, sexual orientation, physical abilities, and more. How you spend your dollars matters. This book will mainly focus on investing money and time, but even if you don't ever invest, your awareness of the types of change happening in the world will be heightened. And you may think of other ways you can make a difference. I hope if you do, you will reach out and share with me what you discovered.

THE FINANCIAL REWARDS AND THE EMOTIONAL ONES TOO

Charity alone can't fix the world's problems. To "be the change," we can invest in the change we want to see in the world. We can do good while doing well. Donating to charity isn't the only way to do good, and traditional investing with stocks and bonds isn't the only way to do well. We can invest our money, time, or expertise and get rewards that make us feel good both physically and emotionally. Financial rewards can come if we surround the entrepreneurs we invest in with the right support and adequate funding. We don't have to sacrifice a financial return just because we want to make an impact. We can help others, drive change, and even strengthen communities with job creation by helping these young companies grow—and we can get financial rewards too.

Companies like Trader Joe's, Home Depot, and Google are now household names, and they all got started with angel funding. Google now employs more than 150,000 people. While these are big companies and early investors made significant gains, they are one-offs, or unicorns, as they are commonly referred to in the start-up world. More common are the many smaller companies being bought and sold that provide attractive returns for angels. According to the ACA, the internal rate of return (IRR) for angel investing is around 27 percent. According to Investopedia, the average rate of return for publicly traded companies in the S&P 500 over the last ten years was less than half that, at 12.4 percent. Investing does come with risk, but it is important to note angels do want to do good in the world, and they also want a financial return as outlined in the graphic on the next page.

Be a Change Angel to *Do Good* while *Doing Well*

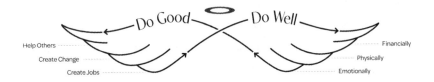

WHAT I WISH I'D KNOWN

One thing I wish I'd had back in 2012 was a strategy for my angel investing.

I invested quite a bit of time and some money without thinking about the big picture and how this would fit into what I really cared about and what change I wanted to see. At the beginning, I was eager to learn, so I would take coffee meetings with just about any entrepreneur. I made time and financial investments without having all the facts. I had "shiny-object syndrome." Or in this case, shiny-*halo* syndrome. I would get involved even if it didn't fit into my "investment thesis." Every money manager, whether of mutual funds or pension funds, has an investment thesis. Experienced investors will have a clear plan that details specifics about what they will and won't invest in. The types of companies, how developed the business is, and how much money they are willing to commit—all these things would go into an *investment thesis*. I didn't know this when I got started. I would see a company or founder I liked and make my decision. This book will help you create your investment thesis, or what we will call your *halo strategy*.

I didn't start with a halo strategy (I wish I had), but what I did have was an amazing mentor, Catherine Mott. She founded the angel investing group BlueTree Allied Angels in Pittsburgh, Pennsylvania, where I went to my first meeting. I learned so much there. The group taught me what makes a company investable as well as the factors that go into helping a company grow. You will learn more about how decisions get made and what happens after you invest.

By being a member of BlueTree, I was also a member of the ACA. The ACA is the professional association of angel investors across the US focusing on education, networking, public policy, and data analytics. In 2012 when I first met Catherine, I had no idea how much I would follow in her footsteps. She advocated for me to be an ACA board member while she was chairing the board in 2015. I not only became a board member, I was also elected as ACA board chair 2021-2023.

Another thing I had was an intense curiosity to explore any "new way" to invest. Early on, these "ways" included investing through funds or platforms, investing as debt versus equity, or focusing on a specific industry or sector—all of which I'll explain throughout the book. This curiosity led to investments I likely wouldn't make today, but I learned so much about what to do and what not to do.

Looking back, what I was missing was a guide I could use ahead of investing time or money. A guide to help me decide what I cared about the most, how much I was willing to contribute both in hours and dollars, and ways I found appealing to increase my exposure to more companies and decrease my risk of losses.

I created a guide for you to use throughout this book called the Halo Strategy™ Worksheet. You can download it at marciadawood.com/dogood.

EXERCISE: IDENTIFYING YOUR START-UP SKILLS

Make a list of the skills you have that could be useful to a start-up. For me, I'm good with spreadsheets and numbers. I have helped a few companies with simple financial projections. I'm also a good listener, and although I'm not a therapist, I have ended up helping company founders just by giving them a shoulder to lean on.

List five skills you have that will add value to a start-up (hint: no skill is too small or too big). And if you aren't sure what your helpful skills could be, ask a friend or family member to help you with your list.

_____

_____

_____

_____

_____

Now take your answers and add them to the "My Valuable Skills" box of the Halo Strategy™ worksheet.

Once you download the worksheet, you can take your answers from the skills exercise you just did and add your answers to the My Valuable Skills box on the worksheet.

Throughout the book, I'll walk you through fun exercises that will help you fill out the worksheet. By the end of the book, you will have a list of personal values, an investing mission and vision statement, an assessment of your risk tolerance, and a list of causes you care about, which will help you decide on your Halo Strategy™. And of course, we will cover ways you can get started on your Be-the-Change journey.

This is the guide I wish I'd had early on to set me on the right path to find the companies creating change that mattered most to me, and to help me develop a plan for finding the financial and emotional rewards I was seeking.

By the time you finish this book, you will have an outline of what you truly care about, the changes you would like to see in the world, and a plan for how to be that change. You will know how you can put your time, money, expertise, or all of the above to work to achieve financial gains, emotional rewards, or both! You will be ready to realize your invest-for-change potential.

When I see the magnet my dad gave me in my office today, I feel proud to have found a way to be the change in my own way through angel investing. I've gotten to see and sometimes even test out really cool products, services, medical treatments, technologies, and more. My bubble of a world has been expanded to include things I didn't even know existed. And I've gotten many different rewards over the years; some of the best ones are simple thank-yous from grateful entrepreneurs who needed someone to believe in them so *they* could be the change they want to see in the world.

Angels are vital in giving entrepreneurs the support they need to achieve bigger and more impactful innovations. What if innovators like Thomas Edison, Ben Franklin, Amelia Earhart, or Steve Jobs had given up? All of them faced several setbacks in their journeys but kept at it. All of them were entrepreneurs with support systems that enabled them to affect the world as we know it today.

Creating change is the responsibility of all of us. Imagine if everyone invested just a small amount of money, time, or expertise to help a young company. There are roughly 330 million people in the US, and 78 percent of them are over eighteen years old—258 million. Imagine if those 258 million people each invested $100. That equals more than $25 billion. Can you imagine what kind of change in the world can be made with $25 billion? We need to start somewhere, and it can start with $100. Now imagine if each of those people invested $100 each year for ten years. That would put $250 billion to work helping to create change. You get the idea—the more that get involved, the bigger the impact, and no one needs to do it alone. While I couldn't find a cure to help my mom, change is happening all around us that could one day save the life of someone you love.

Chapter Two

HOW ANYONE CAN INVEST IN CHANGE

WE ADDRESSED THE ELEPHANT IN THE ROOM briefly in Chapter 1—*Is angel investing just for the rich?* Now you know it is not. Let's drill down on the details of how anyone can do this. As of this writing, two main ways exist for anyone with a bank account or credit card and an internet connection to invest for as little as $50. Equity crowdfunding and revenue-based financing are avenues we can go down now. Likely, by the time you read this book, even more creative opportunities will have come to light. You will also see references to various platforms as you read on. Some of them may still be around, some may be gone, and I'm sure others will emerge.

Go to marciadawood.com/dogood to see an updated list of them all.

Equity crowdfunding, facilitated by the SEC's Regulation Crowdfunding (Reg CF), is the way someone would invest a small amount of money into a company and get a small piece of ownership in return. Revenue-based financing (RBF) allows someone to loan capital in exchange for a percentage of ongoing gross revenues but not actually own any part of the company. Some refer to RBF as "revenue-financed capital" because they don't want RBF for start-ups to be confused with the very short-term merchant-cash-advance community.

We're still in the early days of this exciting shift, but the change is undeniable. Let's begin by demystifying crowdfunding, which began as a novel way to support creative projects and has evolved into a viable means of investing in promising start-ups. I'll explain the origins, the progress, and the potential of this movement. But be warned, there's still a journey ahead before it reaches the ease and transparency of stock-trading platforms like E-Trade or Robinhood. From there, we will examine what RBF is and how it works for both entrepreneurs and investors.

To start, the word *crowdfunding* means exactly that: new products, causes, or companies funded by the crowd. In most cases, *the crowd* could include anyone with the ability to utilize an online platform.

The three most common forms of crowdfunding are:

- Rewards-Based: You get perks or rewards for buying a product or service, usually prior to manufacturing or full availability to the public.

- Donation-Based: You help a person, group, or cause by donating money.

- Equity-Based: You get a small amount of ownership for investing money.

REWARDS-BASED CROWDFUNDING

Imagine going to any part of the world and being able to instantly understand or speak the local language. In 2016, I bought a set of earbuds. Not just any earbuds. These are worn by two people who would not be able to communicate otherwise. As one person speaks in their language, the recipient hears the words in their native tongue. The idea for this invention came when a boy met a girl while traveling, and he wanted to ask her out on a date. However, she spoke French, and he spoke English. He envisioned having a way to talk to her right then and there, without having to take lessons for months. He created a company and began working on the solution. The earbuds link to an app on your phone. As one person talks, the app translates the words being said, and then a computer voice says the words in the other language into the other person's ear. As someone who can only speak English and is very envious of people who can speak multiple languages, I thought these earbuds seemed pretty cool. What a great example of an entrepreneur solving a big problem.

I placed my order for the earbuds on Indiegogo, a rewards-based crowdfunding site, knowing they were likely not going to work perfectly since they were one of the first prototypes. Rewards-based crowdfunding gives companies the opportunity to get products to market early, allowing their backers to pay to test early prototypes and then give feedback. Expectations are set from the beginning on a platform like Indiegogo. When I became a funder, the company told me that the earbuds wouldn't ship for at least six months. I got a discount for being willing to wait, and I was sent updates each month detailing the manufacturing process. The updates let me know six months was going to turn into a year. I didn't mind because the company was very transparent and kept me informed. About a year later, they arrived. These earbuds do work; they are a little clunky, but the version I got is now more than six years old. Over the years since I bought them, I've followed the company's progress. They have advanced the technology and are bringing us closer to a world with no language barriers.

DONATION-BASED CROWDFUNDING

Donation-based crowdfunding allows people to raise money from the public for a personal, charitable, or social cause. Often people will start a campaign to help a family during financial hardship or to mobilize funds to benefit a community project or nonprofit organization. In the past, I supported my friend Robbie Samuels, who started a GoFundMe campaign to support the Transgender Law Center, which according to his GoFundMe site, "changes laws, policy, and attitudes so that all people can live safely, authentically, and free from discrimination regardless of their gender identity or expression." Donation-based crowdfunding sites allow for pretty much anyone to take in donations almost as if they had their own charity. Almost. One key thing to remember is these donations are not tax deductible unless it is clearly stated that the proceeds are going to a 501(c)(3) organization.

In the summer of 2022, the power of crowdfunding brought a spark of hope to a Ukrainian refugee family, showcasing the true spirit of communal support. My friend Hunter Gatewood and his husband, Daniel, found themselves moved to help Alex, Imma, and their one-year-old baby, Nikol, refugees from Odessa,

Ukraine. Understanding the financial burden that lay ahead for the family, Hunter and Daniel turned to GoFundMe. With the simple goal of helping the family start anew in the US—Sonya the cat included—they reached out to the world, and the world responded.

Hunter's neighborhood friend Deirdre recognized another opportunity to harness the power of the crowd. Using Facebook, she orchestrated a campaign to gather essential baby items for Nikol. The response was overwhelming. Donations flowed in from all corners, from baby socks and diapers to precious baby books in Ukrainian. The young mom who donated the fancy stroller? She worked at GoFundMe, highlighting how intricately connected these crowdfunded efforts can be. These two platforms, GoFundMe and Facebook, became the pillars of a community-driven movement.

Crowdfunding through GoFundMe and Facebook was more than a means to an end. It was a way for the community to actively be the change they wanted to see in the world. Every donation, whether of money or essential items, became a real and tangible way for individuals to make a difference. The efforts were more than gestures. They were concrete actions that aligned with the idea of creating a better world.

A year later, the thriving family is evidence that people can bring about significant change when they act upon their beliefs. The community's contributions were not just acts of kindness. They were focused steps toward making the world a more compassionate place. The success of this family stands as proof of what's possible when people decide to be the change they want to see.

The efforts of Robbie, Hunter, Daniel, Deirdre, and all who contributed demonstrated the power of crowdfunding and the principle of being the change. By using these online resources, they translated a concept into action. Their story is a reminder that making a difference is within reach and that the change we want to see in the world starts with our own actions, one step at a time.

Campaigns such as the ones mentioned above can help you on your path to creating change. To see an updated list of active donation-based crowdfunding platforms, visit my website at marciadawood.com/dogood.

EQUITY-BASED CROWDFUNDING

One of the newest forms of crowdfunding, equity-based crowdfunding (Reg CF), offers a small piece of ownership in a company in exchange for an investment of money. This is it—this is the way just about anyone can invest in a start-up for as little as $50. All the best practices of investing in a start-up that we will cover throughout the book also apply here, only now the low entry requirement has opened crowdfunding to a much wider audience. Prior to May 2016, this type of fundraising was not allowed, and it didn't happen overnight. Four years prior, in 2012, President Obama signed the JOBS (Jumpstart Our Business Startups) Act into law. The primary goal was to foster economic growth by making it easier for start-ups and small businesses to raise capital. While it's the job of the president to sign the act into law, it is up to the SEC to formulate and implement the specific rules and regulations governing this type of funding, also referred to as EC. Hence the long stretch of time before it was allowed. Once all the regulations were sorted out, in 2016, this type of investing became accessible to anyone. With equity crowdfunding, the investor doesn't have to meet certain income or wealth requirements of the SEC, as we will learn in Chapter 4. The pool of potential investors is now much larger, and the investment can be as little as $50. Likely the ownership amount received for a $50 investment will be less than a fraction of a percent, but each investor now has a vested stake in helping the company succeed. After personally looking through many equity crowdfunding campaigns, I haven't found many that had minimums as low as $50. Most start at $100, even though the regulations state it can be as low as $50. But again, it is still early days.

WHY COMPANIES CHOOSE TO RAISE MONEY FROM THE CROWD

Typically, the most successful Reg CF fundraising campaigns are by companies with a product or service that can be sold directly to consumers (DTC). Side note—DTC is a term you often hear with start-ups since they usually sell DTC or B2B (business to business). They do well because, in addition to raising capital, they also raise awareness by marketing their product or service on the site. The online platforms Wefunder, Republic, and StartEngine, as of 2024, own most of the equity crowdfunding market share. These websites operate much like e-commerce sites. A start-up company showcases all the details of their offer and explains what they do, how they make money, and who are the people on the management team. They are marketplaces connecting entrepreneurs to potential investors.

Brian Scott is the CEO of PittMoss, a Pittsburgh company making a peat moss substitute from recycled newspaper, allowing plant growers to use less water. Brian is a serial entrepreneur turned angel who stepped in to run the company after he became an investor. Before this, Brian joined RentWay right out of college and helped take them public. Over the next few years, RentWay grew from $7 million in sales to almost $700 million before they sold the company to Rent-A-Center. From there, he and his business partner started their own rent-to-own and short-term lending company. During this time, Brian joined BlueTree Allied Angels. BlueTree members had invested in PittMoss before its founder, Mont Handley, appeared on *Shark Tank* in 2015. He received a $200,000 investment from Mark Cuban, which lent PittMoss some valuable name recognition for having appeared on the show. Fast-forward, Mont and his investors were looking for a permanent CEO. The timing was good, since Brian's company was sufficiently established for his partner to manage it without him, and he had the skill set and tenacity to take PittMoss to the next level.

Since Brian was already an angel with lots of angel friends, you would think it was easy for him to raise capital, right? Wrong. He had a few angels invest early, and people were excited to see someone with Brian's business experience brought in to help commercialize the idea. Still, the operation would need to be more efficient before a larger number of investors would get behind PittMoss. When Brian took over, the company was manufacturing the product only to sell commercially by the truckload. Once the product was available to home gardeners in smaller bags, crowdfunding became more attractive, as the investor could also be the customer and vice versa.

After running the company for a few years, Brian believed he had built up PittMoss enough to make it appealing for his existing customers to become investors. Brian liked the idea of equity crowdfunding. He could get the funding he needed to grow the company and have customers with a vested interest in its success. Imagine the level of brand loyalty you might have for a product like your toothpaste if you were an equity owner. You would likely not just buy the product for yourself but also recommend it to others.

But Brian was worried. Traditional angels don't like equity crowdfunding. Yes, you read that right: angels are not fans of this type of investing. Why? Well, it's complicated. On the surface, this looks great—anyone can be an angel investor for as little as $50. But it takes a lot of fifty-dollar investments to contribute to building a company. That equates to a lot of owners. With each person having such a small percentage of ownership, no one person could demand control, but the venture capitalists (VCs) of the world don't like a lot of small investors on the cap table. Cap table stands for capitalization table, which is simply a list of all the investors and the percentage of the company they own. The VCs don't like a "messy cap table" with many small investors because they worry about the large number of questions they could get or, worse, upset investors who get impatient as the company grows and could file a lawsuit. Angels get scared that if a company raises money with EC, they are limiting their chances of getting funding from bigger VC firms down the road. And not attracting venture funding could lead to the company not growing to a size that could bring big returns.

Brian weighed the pros and cons. Pros: he could get the funding needed to grow the company, get more customers, and build loyalty. He also factored that PittMoss's *Shark Tank* appearance gave them bonus points with potential crowdfunders. Many companies don't have that benefit. Brian was also able to structure the legal documents so that all the crowdfunders would stay off the cap table until there was an exit. Cons: he might limit future funding opportunities from venture investors with deeper pockets. He decided to go for it, but he needed to figure out which online platform would be best. It was 2021, only five years after all the newly minted rules of Reg CF were made available. Still very early days, with only a few platforms able to implement the regulations to the level of the SEC's requirements. He went with Republic.com. That platform showcases a diverse range of investment opportunities, including technology start-ups, consumer products, real estate projects, and more.

Sidenote: An "exit" refers to a liquidity event where founders and investors sell their stakes in the company, ideally making a nice profit. This happens mainly through acquisition by another company. But occasionally this can happen through a merger or by going public through an initial public offering [IPO]. An exit is often the end goal for start-ups and their investors, providing a return on investment and freeing up capital for new ventures.

Raising funds through a Reg CF campaign on a site is not an "if you build it, they will come" type of thing. The onus is on the entrepreneur to get the word out and bring early investors they know to the site to get started. Investors can browse the available investment opportunities on these sites, view company profiles, investment terms, and financial information. They can then choose to invest in promising companies that align with their investment goals. Getting people excited about a company, the product, and the team behind it leads to a snowball effect of more investors participating.

To get set up on the site, Brian needed to provide a pitch deck, the most recent financial statements, and a video summarizing the offer, which is one of the most important elements. And video taken on a phone wouldn't impress anyone; this had to be somewhat professionally done. He needed people to understand the financial and business elements of the company as well as appreciate the social good they would be doing. The SEC is clear about what needs to be disclosed to raise money using Reg CF. The template on Republic was straightforward, and Brian uploaded all PittMoss's details. Being the pro that Brian is, he had it set up in just about two weeks.

Now all the marketing had to begin. He started by asking his current customers and angels to go to the platform and help the campaign by investing. The more traction the company can get at the beginning, the more the platform will expose the campaign to other investors who may not know about the company. Brian pushed out the information on social media and did an email marketing campaign. Within a few months, all the small checks started to add up. They raised $730,000 with a range of check sizes from $100 to more than $1,000.

Brian went all in on this campaign. He did an excellent job communicating with the potential investors right on the platform. You see, the CEO of a start-up raising funds through Reg CF is required to communicate with all investors *on the platform only*. No emails or side conversations. If someone asks a question, even if the question wasn't originally asked on the site, the answer (and question) must be posted for all to see. Brian liked this approach. It was easier to keep track of who wanted to know what. Some people asked very detailed questions, and some were basic. Seeing how a CEO answers questions on the platform can reveal a lot about the character and personality of the leader. I always learn so much about a company and who is running it by reading through the comment section.

Another factor that led Brian to success was his dedication to sharing weekly updates and new information about the company, the product, and their fundraising progress. Often, people begin as followers of a campaign, and as they see more positive updates and new content, they are more likely to convert to investors. Not all companies that use these types of platforms perform the same. The CEO and their team can make or break the campaign. Before investing, it is important to understand the promotion strategy for the campaign's duration. Otherwise, there may not be enough support to take the company forward and get them the needed capital. However, a well-designed plan along with execution, as in the case of PittMoss, can lead to the win-win of customers becoming investors and investors who become lifelong customers.

HOW TO START AS AN INVESTOR

Unlike public stocks, which can be bought or sold at any time, private companies only open opportunities to invest when capital is needed. The potential private company investment options are vast but will look different from day to day. Equity crowdfunding is no exception.

Since Reg CF has only been around since 2016, it's still very early days. We still need to see plenty of innovation for:

- The Platforms: If you google "best equity crowdfunding sites," the results will give you plenty of places to check out. Many, though, assume you know what crowdfunding is before you get there, making the user experience daunting.

- The number of start-ups using EC: While there is an increasing number of start-ups raising capital this way, the number of choices of where to invest is still relatively limited.

- Searching for the change you want to see in the world: Many of the sites don't allow for searching by cause or category. You can search by industry or company size, but if you try to search with something like "cure cancer," you probably won't find what you are looking for.

Now that you know the limitations, the rest can be easy. At any given time, a variety of interesting companies are fundraising on Reg CF sites. Head over to my website at marciadawood.com/dogood to see a list of current Reg CF platforms and to see the closed campaign that PittMoss did on Republic.com in 2021. From there, you can see what companies that are fundraising may fit into your Halo Strategy™.

No matter how you start searching, you are bound to find something that aligns with your goal of making change in the world. Of course, don't forget the golden rule in early-stage investing—look for a while before making an actual investment. You will learn a lot by just browsing. In 2016, I was simply perusing Indiegogo when I found the translation earbuds. I didn't even know that type of technology existed, so I would have never searched for it. Some of the best early companies I've come across were the ones I had no idea about. I wish equity crowdfunding had been around when I started angel investing. The transparency required of the start-ups on these platforms is very educational and can help get you started on this interesting journey.

REVENUE-BASED FINANCING

Revenue-based financing has come into fashion among angel investors over the last few years. So, what exactly is revenue-based financing (RBF)? It's a unique way for growing businesses to receive financial capital in exchange for a percentage of ongoing gross revenues. Often start-ups in the early days aren't producing much revenue. However, those that do have some leverage. In Chapter 7, I will go into more detail on how the traditional angel-group model is being disrupted by RBF, but now we will focus on dipping your toe into the water with small amounts of money. RBF is a unique way to invest for change.

Wefunder, one of the platforms I mentioned above, with a large chunk of the market share for EC, introduced investing through RBF for as little as $100 in January 2023. Justin Renfro, who heads up the Wefunder RBF division, was on *The Angel Next Door* podcast in September 2023. During the show, he explained how it works. His examples tended to be companies in your neighborhood, such as a trendy coffee shop that recently opened down the block. With revenue-based financing, you could invest a small amount of money, like $100, in exchange for a portion of the coffee shop's future revenues. Instead of receiving a percentage of ownership, as we saw with EC, which could take a long time to translate into a return, you'll start receiving regular payments based on the coffee shop's sales. It's a win-win situation because your investment grows as the business thrives, and you get to be a part of the coffee shop's success story.

The beauty of equity crowdfunding generally, and this type of RBF specifically, is that it levels the playing field for investors of all backgrounds. Whether you're a student, a working professional, or a retiree, you can now support local businesses and potential unicorns without breaking the bank. It's a grassroots movement that empowers individuals to invest in the businesses they believe in, making dreams come true one small investment at a time.

Chapter Three

THE HIDDEN TREASURES OF INVESTING IN START-UPS

IN 2021, FASCINATED BY ALL THE REASONS people become angel investors, I started *The Angel Next Door* podcast. On the show, I ask guests to explain how they learned about angel investing and why they do it. It's so interesting to hear everyone's distinct story, as everyone has their own set of reasons for investing. No one has ever told me their reasons are purely financial. Most people are driven by emotional or intrinsic rewards. While financial rewards are self-explanatory, the intrinsic or emotional rewards can be many and have varying degrees of importance or relevance.

Alisha Griffey was a guest who told me she was an entrepreneur before she became an angel. Women get less than 3 percent of the funding that men get. Alisha was so frustrated seeing this reality that she wanted to do something about it. More on Alisha's journey in Chapter 7. Jake Whitman is an angel turned entrepreneur. He wants to see more done to reduce climate change, so he created a company making wine packaged with 55 percent less material and fuel for shipping. He did all this while creating jobs as his company, Really Good Boxed Wine, grows. For discounts on Really Good Boxed Wine and other great stuff start-ups are working on, go to marciadawood.com/dogood.

When I was first learning, I automatically equated investing with financial returns. I had no idea how many other rewards there were. Now I group intrinsic rewards into five buckets. Creating jobs, networking with people outside your career or social circles, personal growth, the good feelings from paying it forward, and getting a first look at some of the cool stuff being created. These are all reasons why people become and continue to be angels. All these reasons matter to me.

JOB CREATION

One of my reasons for starting and continuing to be an angel investor is to contribute to job creation—jobs that people enjoy and allow them to contribute to making the world a better place. While we don't have a lot of data around how many jobs are created because of angel investors, Desert Angels, an angel group in Tucson, Arizona, did a study over a ten-year period showing the economic contribution the investors made. Collectively they invested $47.3 million in ninety-five different companies. The study concluded that "for every $100,000 of investment, these portfolio companies produce 5.8 direct jobs, $458,000 in wages and $2.1 million in economic output." If we do the math, this one angel group over ten years contributed roughly $1 billion to the local economy. This is a real-life example of the old adage about giving someone a fish and feeding them for a day or teaching them to fish and feeding them for a lifetime. This is like creating an entire fishing conglomerate!

At one point, I tried to add up how many jobs got created from the companies I was invested in. It was hard to measure an exact number, but conservatively, I contributed to hundreds if not thousands of jobs being created. I might have been a tiny percent of a percent of the investments into those companies, but I still played a role.

NETWORKING

I had no idea how many people from different industries I would meet as an angel. I have met people through local meetings, larger events, and collaborative decision-making about investing in a start-up. Having a shared goal of deciding to invest in a company is an interesting way to get to know people. You analyze and strategize about the company, the team, the product, or service; who would pay for it; and how much the company could grow, just to name a few. These types of conversations allow you to get to know someone pretty well after just a few weeks. And you work in groups, so no part of the work or decision is left to just one person. Plus, angels get to network with entrepreneurs and all the other investors that invest in a company. I am a co-investor in a company with Mark Cuban. I've co-invested alongside big venture capital firms and other strategic companies like Constellation Brands. I knew of an angel group that was started because the leader of that group was friends with a professional football player. She started an angel group for professional athletes, giving her access to a whole new world of people. While there are stories of angels getting to interact with celebrities, which can be interesting, every angel makes new friends and builds relationships with like-minded people each time they look at a new company for investment.

The network effect also comes when entrepreneurs become serial entrepreneurs after doing well their first time, and they go on to build more companies. If you are an investor at the beginning, you are usually allowed to participate in their later companies, which may be closed off to other investors.

Some people end up becoming angel investors because of their network. Here are a few random examples. A local investor, Quinn, had a sister, Stella, who started a business and was raising what is called a "friends and family" round. This is the very first money raised by a new company. Since Stella knew the founder, she could invest, and likely several other family members and friends would too.

Having a network whose members have attained a certain level of expertise is another way angels get introduced to start-ups. Will is a doctor in gastroenterology, and a company made a product to help doctors during a colonoscopy procedure. Since angels like solving big problems and Will knows firsthand how much this new product could help, he decides to be an investor and back the company.

PERSONAL GROWTH

Learning about all kinds of industries and innovations was one unexpected benefit that I gained from my involvement in angel investing, which has made it worth my investment of time, talent, and resources. Start-ups and entrepreneurs need the expertise and mentorship of angels, but this goes both ways. In my journey, I have learned about different industries I would have never known about. I've seen and experienced the inner workings of a start-up, and I've served on boards of start-ups and helped to navigate their growth. My ability to make decisions and evaluate situations has improved because of the vast amount of exposure I have had to the entrepreneurial environment. Not to mention, start-ups are great cocktail-party conversation; people always like to hear about new and exciting companies or products and services.

I remember seeing a presentation from a company working on enhancing the technology used in the fishing industry. I have no interest in fishing, so I was ready to move on and look at the next company. However, I ended up having several conversations with the founder, and I learned a lot about an industry I knew nothing about, including the large number of people who truly love to fish—from those who do it for a living to the occasional hobbyist. On a few occasions after this experience, I found this knowledge useful in conversations with others. Basically, I was able to hold my own in a fishing conversation.

PAYING IT FORWARD

The reason I hear most often for why people become angel investors is that they want to contribute to the change they want to see in the world, including the kind of change affecting climates, politics, and racism. Watching the news has become a barrage of horrible things happening out in the world. We feel bad, but we are unsure what to do or how to help. So what do we change? The channel.

Change is hard. Big life changes, like changing jobs or relationships, are identified as some of the most stressful events ever to take place in a person's life. Changing our behavior, such as exercising more or eating better, could take weeks to months to years to accomplish—or at least twenty-one days, as some say. We even hesitate with things as simple as relocating to another seat during a meeting or engaging with new people at events.

The number of days between March 15 and March 31, 2020, felt like a hundred! Hearing "shelter in place" for the first time was daunting, and going to the grocery store on March 16 with so many empty shelves was terrifying. I was glued to the television. I was trying to find any semblance of hope during this new pandemic, or at least where to get some toilet paper! During this time, actor John Krasinski aired his first episode of *Some Good News*, showcasing people all over the world cheering and celebrating their local health-care workers on the front lines of the pandemic. We were all craving a way to feel happier during this scary time.

In my own search, I stumbled upon a happiness class, a free, ten-week, online Yale course taught by Dr. Laurie Santos, called *The Science of Well-Being*. Maybe I was influenced by the events of the world around me, but I was engrossed in the learnings. The research showed that subjects would rate themselves on their level of happiness based on a variety of factors. Winning the lottery was among events that brought a short-term spike in happiness, but after a period of time, the winners were no more or less happy than they had been prior to the event. In contrast, the course also included the happiness level of people with quadriplegia who reported their happiness levels were not that far off from those of nondisabled people.

What Dr. Santos came to uncover is that we tend to overestimate external factors, such as material possessions and wealth, and underestimate internal factors, such as health, relationships, and mindset. The other thing the course teaches is that happiness requires intentional effort. Practicing gratitude, building and engaging in strong social connections, and maintaining vibrant physical and mental health are all ways to increase one's happiness.

One of the exercises Dr. Santos gives during weeks seven through ten is practicing random acts of kindness. This could be anything from holding the door for someone, giving a stranger a compliment, or, in an example from Krasinski's first episode, a man mowed his neighbor's grass while the neighbor was deployed overseas. Dr. Santos showed that generosity and giving increase our overall happiness. The pay-it-forward mentality!

Prior to angel investing, I would hear the term "random acts of kindness" or "pay it forward" and think, *I'd like to do more of that*, but it seemed in the periphery of my thinking—not necessarily on my weekly to-do list. After becoming angels, the desire to pay it forward shifted more into focus for Izzy and me. Some acts are things like tipping 25 percent or more to a server instead of the standard 15 percent or going out of our way to shop at a local business.

My good friend and neighbor, Katie Weeks, started doing "birthday givebacks" with her kids from a very young age. In lieu of traditional toys and games as birthday gifts, the children pick a charity or school to donate to and find out what they need.

One year, it was supplies such as coloring pencils, notebooks, and calculators for a local school. Instilling these values as Katie is in her children when they are so young warms my heart, thinking about what they will give back as they grow up.

We don't usually see if the effect of paying it forward made someone else act, but we believe that putting good out into the world is what matters. While living in Pittsburgh, Izzy and I knew Jason, the chef at a local restaurant. Jason invited a group of about eight students from a nearby high school culinary program to look behind the scenes one night when he knew the restaurant would not be overly busy. As the students were all aspiring chefs themselves, they were excited to see the kitchen of a restaurant they knew in action. Jason talked to the students about how he became a chef, gave them a tour of the kitchen, and even allowed them to do some prep work with staff members. Later that week, Jason got several letters from the students expressing their gratitude, but one letter, from student John, stood out. John said this opportunity provided him with clarity on his decision to pursue a culinary career.

Angel investing is a great way to pay it forward. With the goal in mind of getting a financial return while making positive changes, this could lead to a cycle of investing where returns from one investment fund the next.

Now, if we put this all together, we want to be happy, and there are issues or causes in the world where we want to see change. We can be intentional about how we do this. Imagine if everyone created a way to be just a little bit happier, and the changes we want to see in the world started happening bit by bit. It might not be Peace on Earth, but it's a start!

People want change. They say they want to do things to make change, but they don't know how to go about it. People want to be happy, but happiness doesn't happen by accumulating material things; happiness comes from within us. By intentionally forming a "be-the-change plan," you will derive satisfaction by helping the causes you care about, since this level of intentionality is itself part of the wiring in our brains that makes us happier. The be-the-change plan = happiness.

FIRST LOOK

Early access to innovation is another reason to be an investor. I remember watching the first few companies pitch early on and thinking, *How cool that I get to learn about all this before everyone else*. Over the years I've been given the opportunity to try all kinds of new products and services. Everything from different foods, vitamins, skincare, and makeup to human-resources and email software—all before it was offered to a broader market. Heather Henyon, founder of Mindshift Capital, became an investor in Rebel Girls, a book, podcast, and app company highlighting stories of extraordinary women of the past. Their target market is girls between the ages of seven and fourteen, as they want to be the new Girl Scouts of modern times. When Heather first invested, the company only had a few books. She got an inside look at all the new products being worked on before Rebel Girls ended up on "Oprah's Favorite Things."

ONE COMPANY HIGHLIGHTS ALL THE WHYS

Martha Carlin is the founder and CEO of the BioCollective and Biotiquest. Biotiquest makes a line of targeted probiotics to restore gut health.

Here's Martha's story in her own words:

I'm Martha Carlin. In 2002, my forty-four-year-old husband, John, was diagnosed with Parkinson's disease. We were told Parkinson's is a disease with no cure and a guarantee of decline over time. The resources provided were limited, John was sent home with a pill to mask the symptoms, and our lives changed forever. Still we were not willing to accept defeat or the status quo approach to the disease.

My business career was as a systems thinker and turnaround expert, so I began to apply those turnaround skills to the puzzle of Parkinson's disease. I immediately began my quest to find a cure. In the meantime, I worked to find ways to help John better manage and improve other aspects of his health to improve his Parkinson's prognosis. I looked at food choices, nutrition, chemical exposures through the diet, and more. We changed our diet over the years as more research began to support the importance of diet and nutrition in all chronic diseases. Over the years the research began to build and connect until, in 2014, the first research was published pointing to the gut.

This was my eureka moment! From my business lens, I could see the gut as the general ledger for our health, the record of what is flowing through the system.

I quit my job, and we started funding research at the University of Chicago with Dr. Jack Gilbert. Through that research, I learned how many chronic diseases are connected to gut bacteria. I founded the BioCollective to help bring together people and research to get the data needed to connect the dots across diseases through the bacteria and their metabolic functions in the gut. Since I founded the company and became a recognized opinion leader in Parkinson's, many people have been contacting me to find out how they could improve their prognosis. I fielded calls and emails but ultimately decided it was time to make my knowledge more easily accessible.

Martha is truly an inspirational entrepreneur. She is not a doctor, nor does she have a PhD. She saw a big problem and set out to solve it. She is the kind of entrepreneur who checks all the boxes we just reviewed on reasons to invest in a start-up.

- Job Creation: She has created jobs by building her company.

- Networking: She has a vast network of contacts and is generous with introductions.

- Personal Growth: I, along with others she knows, have learned so much from her work over the years, adding to our personal growth.

- Paying it Forward: She found a huge problem not just for the world, but especially for her family: curing Parkinson's disease.

- First Look: I was lucky enough to get a first look at her product when she first started making the probiotic, and she would send me samples from the lab.

Martha was directly affected by a big problem, her husband's diagnosis of Parkinson's disease (PD). She went on a quest to find a solution and along the way discovered so many more things. While Martha does not officially have a PhD, her knowledge level of the microbiome and the body's overall systems is off the charts. She has read an impressive number of scientific white papers and went so far as to create her own bank of stool samples from both PD patients and non-PD subjects. She is affectionately known as "the poop lady." But her research has paid off in spades. As of this writing, her husband, John, is doing well, and his disease progression has slowed because of Martha's efforts.

I was particularly interested in Martha's work because of my mom's ALS diagnosis and my own quest to make sure I did not see ALS in my future. I was thrilled when Martha and her team of scientists developed the probiotic and made it available across the US. While the probiotic is not a cure, I believe it is a product promoting good health.

Martha is an example of someone putting all their time, money, and talent into finding a way to "be the change you want to see in the world." However, everyone who has helped Martha or any of the other countless start-ups working on change, whether the contribution was big or small, is creating their own version of being the change.

LET'S NOT FORGET ABOUT MONEY

While this chapter does focus primarily on the intrinsic or emotional reasons or rewards for angel investing, money is also an important reason. However, if my only goal were to make money, I might focus primarily on public-market investing. And if my only goal were to feel good about helping others, I might set up a foundation and raise money to give away. Angel investing is somewhere in the middle, but it is not charity! Angels *do* want a financial return.

What I find a bit frustrating is when the terms *angel* and *impact* are used interchangeably related to investing. Let's debunk the myth that impact investing is charity.

According to Investopedia, the definition of *impact* investing is "an investment strategy that aims to generate specific beneficial social or environmental effects in addition to financial gains."

This is an accurate definition, and as an angel, I like it. However, there is a perception among the overall financial community that "impact investing" will result in lower or no financial returns.

Also, "aiming to generate specific beneficial social and environmental effects" means making an impact. So here, *impact* means making change.

Not all angels invest in start-ups doing good in the world. Some start-ups work on improving tobacco, fossil fuels, drug paraphernalia, and more. My frustration comes when an angel is investing in a company that *is* doing good and gets the label of an "impact investment." It is by definition an impact investment. However, it gets looked at as if it were charity and no financial returns are expected. That is simply not true. There are many start-ups working on ways to improve our planet and health care, and they aren't doing this out of the goodness of their hearts. They are working toward a financial return. A sustainable business model allowing the start-up to grow and thrive over the long-term is the key to being able to have both.

An example that can be found in most grocery stores would be household and personal care products by Seventh Generation. This company uses sustainable and plant-based ingredients. They are a for-profit company doing good and making money.

Angels do want to make money and do good, which is why we have such shiny halos.

EXERCISE: UNCOVER YOUR PASSION!

Jot down the causes that ignite your heart. What are the changes you want to see in the world? I'm partial to gender equality, clean water, and anything helping people with neuromuscular diseases like ALS.

Your causes:

_____

_____

_____

_____

Now take your answers and add them to the "Changes I want to see in the world" box of the Halo Strategy™ worksheet.

Chapter Four

UNDERSTANDING THE PROCESS OF INVESTING IN A START-UP

As Izzy and I walked through downtown Pittsburgh on a dreary day in February 2012 to our first angel investing meeting, I said, "Do you think this meeting will be like those investment groups who pick stocks together?"

"No," he said. "This is about investing in private companies, not public ones."

"Oh. Do you know how much people invest?"

"No idea."

"Do we have to invest or pay anything today?"

"No. We are guests today. We can see what we think."

"OK." I paused, then added, "And don't get too excited about investing until we have all the details."

I say this because Izzy and I have different levels of risk tolerance when it comes to money. His dad, a global commodities trader, lost a significant amount of money in 1980 when the silver market crashed, dropping the price over 80 percent in two months. It took over ten years for him to get back to those precrash levels, moving the family to three different countries during Izzy's teenage years. The lessons learned from his dad included not going all in on one investment, investing in the things you believe in, not being afraid to fail, and understanding that big risks can mean big rewards. My upbringing was different. I grew up in a modest household where my dad would teach me every month about budgeting as he paid the family expenses. I learned a little about stocks at a young age and was taught to be cautious.

Walking into the meeting, I was curious but slightly nervous because I had no idea if we could afford to be angel investors. I didn't know what to expect and worried that I might look foolish if I asked a question.

Wow, these are fancy offices, I thought as I stepped off the elevator. I had to check in with security just to get up to the forty-second floor.

The paper sign taped to the glass door read: BlueTree Allied Angels Meeting. I noticed the permanent sign on the wall was for a law firm.

"Marcia and Izzy, please come sit here at the main table for the meeting," Catherine Mott, CEO of BlueTree, warmly greeted us.

About forty people sat in the large conference room, mostly men; I counted five women. Another couple, also new, were in their thirties. Izzy and I were in our early forties and together, we were bringing down the average age in the room. There was an agenda at each seat on this U-shaped table setup. About fifteen people could sit "up front" at the table, and there were chairs behind it for others to sit. I later learned those chairs are for nonmembers and students who were there for educational purposes; the investors sat up front. I found it interesting that

there were so many students there to learn.

The agenda showed there would be two companies presenting, or "pitching." The first was a medical device company making a respiratory dialysis machine called Alung. I'm not a science person and I was not familiar with respiratory dialysis, but the CEO did a nice job explaining to us nonscience people that they were working on an artificial lung. He began with a story about a person who was on the waiting list for a lung transplant. This patient was not well enough to get the transplant, and doctors worried that if they tried the surgery, the patient would not make it. The Alung machine could be used for a short time (one to two weeks) and could improve the patient's lung function to be stronger for the transplant surgery. While the working prototype had been approved for "emergency use," the regulatory approvals needed to begin manufacturing and selling were a long way off. As someone who had worked over the last twenty years for big corporations, I was fascinated as I learned about the start-up world.

During the roughly ten uninterrupted minutes the CEO was given, he explained the business, the Food and Drug Administration (FDA) approval strategy, the financials, their exit potential, and "the offering." The offering is a little like what we hear on *Shark Tank*: "XYZ company is looking for $250,000 for 20 percent of their company." It's the offering of the opportunity to invest in the company in which the terms of the investment are spelled out.

ANGEL INVESTING ON TV

Many of you have seen *Shark Tank,* which has given people a loose frame of reference for what angel investing is.

In theory, what you see on TV is angel investing. On the show, an entrepreneur walks in and says something like, "I'm looking for $200,000 for 20 percent of my company." Just for easy math, that means the company would be valued at $1 million, because $200,000 is 20 percent of $1 million.

The sharks evaluate and decide if what they are seeing is worth $1 million. They will decide if they are in or out based on factors such as:

- Do they like the industry?
- Do they believe people will buy/use the product?
- Do they believe these are the right people to grow this company?
- Is there a big enough market to sell the product?
- Does the company already have a certain amount of revenue?

On TV, this looks like it is done in a matter of minutes. In reality, the due diligence process of evaluating a company to see if we want to invest takes weeks and even months to complete.

I heard many financial, manufacturing, and FDA requirement terms, just to name a few—that were new to me. It seemed a bit overwhelming. Immediately after the presentation, we had ten minutes as a group to ask questions of the team. At this point, I had about a thousand questions, most of which I thought were silly, so I didn't raise my hand. I figured I didn't know enough yet to ask anything.

I whispered a couple of questions to Izzy. I thought, *He is in finance, he should understand some of these terms.*

He whispered back, "These are angel-investing terms, so I'm not sure."

"Angel speak" became a coined phrase in our household. The questions the other members asked focused mainly on the investment terms—not as many questions about the product, the FDA process, or the manufacturing and commercialization, which I found odd. *How do we know if this product actually works?*

When time was up for the Q&A, the CEO and team were asked to leave the room while the group discussed if the company was worthy of a closer look for investment. Catherine started by asking what everyone liked about the company. The team was very experienced, and the CEO had led a company to a successful exit in the past. The FDA emergency-use authorization of the device was looked at favorably.

Then Catherine asked what people disliked. The general consensus among the group was the amount of capital needed to build this product and get the company to a successful exit would be very high and take a long time, even with all the progress that had been made. But overall, the pros outweighed the cons, and the company was voted to move on to the "due diligence phase," which meant a much deeper dive would be done on the details of the company. This allowed the group to get a closer look so investors could make a final decision about writing a check.

Then we saw company number two, PittMoss. You will remember this company from Chapter 2, but this was long before they did a crowdfunding campaign. And as a reminder, they make a peat moss substitute out of recycled newspaper, allowing plant growers to use less water. I was thinking, *Company number one is working to save humans, and company number two is trying to save the planet. Nice.* We went through the same process, hearing from this company before the group voted to move into the due diligence phase.

The meeting ended with some time to socialize, where we could meet the company CEOs and team members. I hadn't been willing to ask questions in the main session, but I felt more comfortable in the one-on-one setting. I asked company number two about how they were making the product. The answer the CEO gave was confusing. A few minutes later I was talking to another member of the angel group, Paul, who knew the company fairly well. He told me the manufacturing wasn't very efficient yet because they were still optimizing the process and could only make small batches at a time. Start-ups have many constraints. They are small and run most of the business on a shoestring budget. I had no experience with such small companies, but I was fascinated at the big innovations being worked on to make significant change in the world.

Paul said, "New members often ask the best questions, so don't be shy about speaking up."

"Really?" I asked. "I thought that because I'm new and don't know about angel investing, I should let the others, who know more, ask the questions."

"No question is a silly question, and it takes the wisdom of many people to figure out if an investment should be made into a start-up." He went on to explain that sometimes experienced angels get bogged down in the details, and a fresh set of eyes can look from a higher level, which helps the overall process of evaluating the company.

At the end of the night, I felt like I had a lot to learn, but I was energized to get involved and learn more about all these interesting companies. I'd lived in Pittsburgh for over twenty years, and I had no idea so much was happening right in my own backyard. I thought innovation happened only in big cities.

Chances are good that entrepreneurs are in your neck of the woods too. Start-up events happen in big cities and small towns. To find them, you can simply do an online search of "start-up events in _____ (insert your city or town)." You can get started by just listening and asking questions and seeing what fun, innovative things are happening in your backyard.

A BRIEF HISTORY OF ANGEL INVESTING

One of the things that helped me in the early days was learning some of the history of how angel investing got started, the details of how it evolved, and what happened to get people interested in start-ups. Wealthy individuals financially backing theater productions was the origin of angel investing.[3] An *angel* is someone using their own money to invest in a private company at an early stage. The angel groups of today began to form in the early 2000s. Through the 2010s, investing through venture capital or angel funds, donor advised funds (DAFs), and equity crowdfunding gained popularity, as will be discussed in later chapters.

Over the next several years, I had the opportunity to learn how other angel groups and even individual angels around the country operate. While factors like size, geography, fee structure, access to deal flow, and visibility all vary, the process followed to vet companies is similar. Companies pitch, and investors do their due diligence and decide to invest or not—pretty simple. This is the traditional way to invest in a company, which usually requires an average minimum investment of somewhere around $5,000 to $20,000.

While I was learning the inner workings of the traditional angel world, as we can call it, I also explored the not-so-traditional ways to support start-ups—ways like equity crowdfunding and revenue-based finance that we covered in Chapter 2. I was also learning more about funds and how to pool money up front to invest in multiple companies, allowing me to invest in more companies with less money out of pocket. More on this in later chapters, especially Chapter 9.

Understanding the different models available to help support start-ups and how they work helped me to envision a world where just about anyone could contribute to impactful change. Many people are unfamiliar with this, and it took me considerable time to grasp because private markets—where these early-stage companies operate—offer different types of information compared to what's available for public and established companies. This often leads to the false perception that there's a lack of transparency in the private markets. The reporting regulations for private companies are very limited, which is a big reason why it is hard to get information and why we get that nontransparent feeling about the entire private-market space. We hear more and know more about public companies. So let's start there by looking at how the public markets have gotten to where they are today.

PUBLIC VERSUS PRIVATE COMPANIES

Start-up companies do not have a marketplace to trade shares like public companies have with the US stock markets. A private company's ownership details are therefore often unknown or hard to find out because there is no requirement to disclose this information. So how do people become investors in start-ups? It is usually because they know someone. To understand where we are now with private companies, let's look at the evolution of public companies.

Back in the 1970s and 1980s, if someone wanted to buy public company stocks, they needed to contact a brokerage firm like Morgan Stanley. An account would need to be opened and money wired before a broker would talk directly to the potential investor. Only then would Morgan Stanley contact a "market maker" on the trading floor, who would quote the price, and if accepted, a trade would be placed. The broker charged a fee of a minimum of $100 or a percentage of the trade. This typically took several days or longer. It was an involved process just to buy one stock. This was also a process that only the wealthy could afford.

With the internet, the ability to get quotes became electronic with firms like Charles Schwab. After quotes came the ability to enter trades electronically. The fees came down. Now you can get the same service for free. Today, anyone with internet access and a bank account can buy shares on E-Trade or Robinhood in less than a few minutes.

According to Forbes, less than 1 percent of the twenty-seven million companies in the US are public. And the number of public companies has been declining in recent years, likely due to several factors, including the high cost of listing on an exchange, the increasing complexity of financial reporting requirements, and the growing popularity of alternative sources of capital, such as private equity and crowdfunding. There are a lot of private companies out there!

When I think about how far the public markets have come, I get excited to think about where the private markets can go. But it will be a long road to get there.

In today's world of private companies:

- While it has gotten better since the 1990s and 2000s, angels have less access to investment opportunities than the big Silicon Valley investors.

- Once an investment is made, there are very few options to liquidate or get out of the investment until the company is sold.

- When investors find a company they would like to invest in, they share their thoughts and research with other potential investors, but it is very fragmented.

In an ideal world:

- Access to investing in private companies would be as transparent as investing in the public market—equal access to all companies for everyone.

- There would be the opportunity to buy and sell shares of a private company as quickly and easily as for public stocks.

- All research and discoveries made during the due diligence process of deciding about investing would be shared by all and with all.

WHAT'S THE DIFFERENCE BETWEEN ANGEL INVESTING AND VENTURE CAPITAL?

Angels and venture capitalists (VC) are investors who invest in private companies. However, there are some significant differences between them.

- Investor Profile: Angels use personal funds to invest, while VCs are managers of other people's money. Examples of those other people, or limited partners (LP), as they are called, would be ultra-high-net-worth individuals, endowments, or pension funds.

- Investment Size: Angels write smaller checks to invest since the money comes from their own accounts. VCs tend to have millions, if not billions, of dollars to manage.

- The Stage of the Company: Angels invest in companies when they are very small and getting started. VCs invest when a company has grown and has a higher number of customers or higher revenues.

- Involvement: Both angels and VCs will sometimes become mentors or advisors to companies they invest in. Involvement may include taking a role on the board of directors. According to the ACA, their sixteen thousand members volunteer over one million hours a year to mentor entrepreneurs.

- Patience: Both angels and VCs want financial returns, but angels tend to be more patient than VCs. VCs have LPs they need to report to about their performance. Their goal is to select the companies with the best financial returns in the shortest amount of time.

Since VCs are measured solely on their performance as managers and they control large sums of money, they often decide the value of the company they are investing in. From the *Shark Tank* example earlier in the chapter, a VC may say they want 40 percent of the company for $200,000 instead of the 20 percent the entrepreneur would like to sell.

For a quick and fun, yet educational video about the difference, visit my website to see my Angel Investor vs. Venture Capitalist Rap Battle video at marciadawood.com.

IS ANGEL INVESTING ONLY FOR THE RICH?

As we discussed in Chapter 2, there is a common perception that to be an angel, you need to be rich. Let's drill down on one of the reasons for this perception. The SEC has guidelines around who can participate in certain types of investments. When it comes to investing in private companies, the investor must meet the accredited investor definition. The SEC set up this definition to ensure that people who invest have the financial means to bear the risks involved. We will go over risks in detail in Chapter 9.

The accredited investor definition as it stands today is based mainly on income and wealth levels. The investor must make an annual income of $200,000 if single ($300,000 with a spouse) or have $1 million in net worth, excluding the primary home. A few years ago, the definition was expanded slightly to include a few measures of sophistication such as certain financial licenses. Go to my website at marciadawood.com/dogood for the most recent updates to the definition.

There are so many things wrong with this definition. While I understand the SEC wanting to protect consumers from losing too much money, the gatekeeping here could be expanded. Here are a few reasons why:

- Having money doesn't magically make someone smart enough to know if an investment is good.

- The income of people living on the coasts can be very different from those in the middle of the country.

- Focusing on income alone doesn't factor in size of household and other expenses.

- Anyone can go to a casino to gamble any amount of money or buy unlimited lottery tickets without restraint.

ELI'S $20,000 REASON

Public policy work directly influences the environment in which entrepreneurs and angel investors operate, determining the ease and viability of starting and growing businesses. The ACA is continuously working to educate our legislators, regulators, and key government officials about how investments in start-ups help spur economic growth and create jobs. This is done mainly through relationship building by visiting with members of Congress, their regulator counterparts, and senior administration officials who implement policy. This takes many forms, including visits in Washington, DC, and in congressional home districts, but it can also be in the form of testimony or advocacy papers.

One recent example of this is when my good friend and my fellow ACA board member, Eli Velasquez, testified at a congressional hearing in February 2023. The entire hearing was focused on the pros and cons of the accredited investor definition. Eli had his own story to tell, and he was armed with information from ACA's CEO Pat Gouhin; our government relations firm, Gray Robinson; our public policy committee; and our legal advisory council. This strategy proves to be very successful in influencing outcomes to help the community and to prevent changes that could harm the good work being done in local communities across the country.

Eli started off as an engineer and then went to law school to become an IP attorney, where he first heard the term *angel investor*. He recounted in his testimony: "I had a wealthy friend and successful entrepreneur who told me about his involvement with a group in Southern California and the wealth and income requirements to be an angel. Hearing his recount, I felt like being an angel investor was completely unattainable for me."

In his testimony Eli shared a multitude of activities he was involved in related to early-stage investment, including cofounding a binational technology company to help start-ups, starting angel groups in rural areas of Texas, and working with local universities' technology transfer offices to promote the commercialization of technology being developed there. All these activities would allow him to evaluate early-stage companies and start-ups and decide if he wanted to invest in them.

He stated in his testimony: "At this stage in my career, I had evaluated thousands of deals, vetted hundreds as viable investment opportunities, and partnered with dozens of angel and venture investors, and still I could not participate despite now being more financially secure and only about $20,000 from the accredited investor income threshold. One particular member in our group was a young twenty-something professional who was brand new to angel investing. Despite not having any experience in angel investing, he leveraged his family's trust fund to achieve accredited investor status. He began writing checks and achieved a couple of exits within a couple of years, enough to buy a new house and put his kids in private school. I could not help but feel downtrodden to see wealth simply pass me up so easily despite my deep expertise in the angel investing space and accredited investor status so close within reach."

Finally, in 2020, he was able to finally write his first check after over twenty years as he now qualified under the accredited investor definition.

"It was also at this stage in 2020, over twenty years since my days as a rocket scientist, IP expert, nonprofit founder, university executive, founder of angel groups all over the world and evaluator of tens of thousands of deals that I was finally . . . *finally* able to write my *first* check as an accredited investor. Twenty-two years. I have missed a generation's worth of investment opportunities because I could not participate in the accredited investor asset class. What if I had formal investor education, investment safeguards according to my income or net worth, and professional organizations to mentor me through the investor journey twenty-two years ago? How many exits could I have had? How many small businesses in Southern California, El Paso, Lubbock, Massachusetts, and even Claycomo, Missouri could I have invested in? How many jobs could I have helped create? How many more nonprofit organizations could I have donated to? How much more would I have been able to contribute to the economy?"

This is an important topic, and we need to keep talking about it and educating our legislators to make sure everyone—including people of all genders, races, and socioeconomic levels—have access to investing in private companies as long as they have been educated on the risks.

Eli's story is a real example of how the accredited investor definition has prevented willing investors from participating in this asset class. As of early 2024, the definition still has not changed. However, the ACA has submitted a proposal to the SEC to become the go-to place to receive an overall angel education and certificate reflecting knowledge of the risks.

INVESTOR PROTECTIONS FOR EQUITY CROWDFUNDING

As we learned in Chapter 2, equity crowdfunding has opened an avenue for people who do not meet the accredited investor definition to participate.

The reason why anyone, regardless of income, wealth, or smarts can go onto a trading platform like E-Trade and buy public stocks is because the SEC requires heavily regulated financial disclosures so that the investor knows everything they can about the public company before buying stock. Do you think everyone who ever bought a stock read through all those documents? Have you? Many lawyers get paid well to make sure all those documents contain the proper information. Public companies are big and can afford the lawyers and accountants needed to publish the required financials. Private companies generally don't have this capability. So how did the SEC decide to protect the investor with equity crowdfunding? As of this writing, here are some of the guardrails:

- Limits: There is a maximum amount of money someone can invest if they do not meet the accredited investor definition. As of this writing, according to their website, the income amount the SEC picked was $124,000. If you make less than that, you can only invest the greater of either $2,500 or 5 percent of your salary. If you make more than that, you can invest 10 percent of your income or net worth, up to $124,000.

- Disclosures: Companies need to provide statements about their financials, the management team, how they will use the funding (use of proceeds), the business model, and any potential risks. Also, no *forward-looking* statements are allowed, which means they can't say anything about what they plan to do in the future. This can be tricky since the CEO needs to show the vision of the company.

· Stakeholder vetting: All significant stakeholders in the company need to have completed a background check, with results available to investors for review on the platform.

· Ongoing reporting: Investors are entitled to receive ongoing communications from the company about how they are doing and their financial position.

FEELINGS ABOUT MONEY

When the accredited investor definition is discussed, feelings come up around money. I remember when Izzy and I were first invited to an angel group meeting, we had to acknowledge that we met the accredited investor definition. This felt strange. As if we had to prove our worthiness to go to this meeting based on our level of income or wealth. This is why I don't want the definition to be focused just on money. Just because someone has money doesn't magically make them a smart investor. Seems like a dumb rule. Shouldn't more education be involved?

If we all talked about money more openly, it would not seem strange to have a conversation about how much or how often someone invests. Money can be a difficult topic to discuss as everyone has their own relationship with it. If someone has what is viewed as a lot of money, they are judged; if someone doesn't have much money, they are judged. Rarely is there a happy medium. No matter the size of one's wealth, there is always someone with more and someone with less. We need to be talking about money more often so we, as a society, learn how to better communicate around this vital issue.

Today the amount of education kids get in school about personal finance is next to nothing, yet it is a critical life skill. We need to empower our youth with tools to build wealth and be able to go out and make the world a better place. When I was a young girl, long before online banking, my dad would collect the bills as they came in the mail throughout the month. Toward the end of the month when bills were coming due, he would sit with me and explain budgeting and where all the money he and my mom made went. At the time I had no idea how valuable those budgeting lessons would be later in life and how lucky I was to have someone explaining personal finances to me in such detail. My hope is more people will find out about and get involved with early-stage companies and then get their children involved as well.

When I learned about angel investing and started seeing cool companies, my excitement level was high. I remember thinking, *I want to use all my extra money to invest in start-ups!* And the excitement is still there even many years later. I am fortunate that Izzy and I have similar views toward investing and how we use our money. And we talk about how each of us values the way we use money. For example, one day Izzy told me he wanted to buy a new putter for golf. I don't golf, so my first reaction was "you already have a putter," which is a typical I-don't-play-golf type of statement from me. People who are good at a sport usually want to buy new equipment to improve their game. Once Izzy and I talked about the value of the purchase related to what was in our budget, we came to an agreement. We approach investing the same way. We look at what we value and what is in our budget and talk through whether a particular investment makes sense.

This is not the case for everyone. I have seen many people decide not to invest at all or to invest at very low levels because their spouse either didn't understand or didn't agree to making the investment. Money issues can be among the hardest issues to overcome in a marriage and is one reason why many marriages end in divorce. I have also seen situations where one spouse handles all the finances and the other has no interest in getting involved. This can also be difficult in the event one spouse passes away, leaving the other to manage the finances. We need to talk about money more often!

In 2018, I was working with my friend and colleague, Heather Henyon, on raising the venture fund, Mindshift Capital, to support female founders (more on that in the next chapter). We approached countless people, mainly women, with our idea and our personal investment history. Several people told us, "My husband handles the investing." I find this frustrating because we will not change the small percentage of dollars going to female founders until we get more women sitting at the table on the investor side. Regardless of whether they ever become angel investors, everyone should know about and have a say in their own personal finances. I have seen too many people end up divorced or otherwise on their own and have no idea how to handle their new financial situation. Talking about money is important with all members of your family. If you aren't already, start those conversations today. Go to my website, marciadawood.com/dogood, for a bonus guide, *How to Start Conversations About Money*.

When it comes to how to think and feel about money related to angel investing, investing $50 or $250 is one thing, but how about investing $20,000 or $250,000 as you build your portfolio? Now the stakes have changed, and the conversations need to be much different. This is the main reason I encourage all new angels to take the time to "just watch." Like people browse for cars or houses, be an observer and see many different companies before even considering an investment. And not just a quick glance; review the pitch materials and do some due diligence on ten or even twenty companies before investing. This will take time, and that's OK. Maybe even up to six months or a year, and that's also OK. Start-ups work at lightning speed, and they will tell you they have some incredibly tight deadlines, but there will always be start-ups to invest in, so don't get overwhelmed. It is better to observe and learn and invest wisely (or as wisely as you can) than to rush and regret.

Taking this time can help make the discussion with your partner much easier and fun too. More and more I've had couples tell me how much their evening dinner conversations have changed since learning about angel investing and how they are talking about things they have never talked about before.

In the past, financial advisors used to look at angel investing as "a cute hobby" or just too risky to partake in. Many financial advisors are financially compensated for the products they sell. Therefore, they may not be aligned with what a client wants and can be a wet blanket on any newfound interest in helping start-ups. Plus, financial advisors are also compensated by the volume of assets under their management (AUM). Angel investments are not typically under these advisors' management and, to the contrary, money to fund angel investments is often pulled from the accounts they manage. The resulting AUM decrease means lower fees for them. Over the last few years, the willingness of advisors to engage with alternative assets has slowly started to change for the better, because investors are demanding more options for long-term growth.

Including your financial advisor in your discussions about being an angel investor early on can be very helpful. Don't try to hide it; be open about what you want to do and why. Find your why and think about your long-term strategy to invest in the change you want to see in the world.

HOW CAN WE HIT "THE TIPPING POINT"?

Chapter 2 demystified equity crowdfunding, which allows people regardless of socioeconomic levels to invest in early-stage companies.

I had no idea when I walked into that first meeting in 2012 that I would learn so much so quickly about angel investing, which I had never heard of before. Angel investing has a long way to go to get to the transparency level of investing in public companies, but I'm excited to see the inclusivity increase as much as it has over the last few years. We need to involve everyone to see significant change in the world. Angel investing used to be gated to allow only the wealthy to participate, but not anymore. Just thinking about the idea of more and more people participating in building companies creating change makes me extremely excited. Why? Because I have gotten tired over the years of there not being enough people supporting these companies, leading to their failure. To make matters worse, the technology, treatment, or product they invented often ends up not making it to market, so it is unavailable to help those who truly need it.

Let's break this down further. The primary reason start-ups fail is that they run out of money. And they run out of money because they are not surrounded by the right financial and operational support. In many cases, not enough people knew about the company, what they were working on, or that investment was even an option for them. We have a long way to go to hit a tipping point, that critical juncture where a few investors become many, enabling the concept of angel investing to be more mainstream. We've witnessed this transition in other sectors, such as ride-hailing apps. Initially, both riders and drivers faced challenges in connecting with each other. But as more people embraced these services, the barriers broke down, paving the way for increased adoption and enhanced use by many.

I have made it part of my mission to help push us to that tipping point where finding and investing in companies making significant change is frictionless. This ideal world would have easy-to-navigate places to find the types of companies that people want to back. Every year, we get a little closer to this world as transparency and accessibility improve, but we are far from the world I'm imagining. Remember the example from Chapter 1: if every US adult (258 million people) invested $100 each year for ten years, that would put $250 billion to work, helping create change. This pool of funds could be the lifeline many innovative companies need.

As I think back to when I walked into that first meeting and how many angels and start-ups I've met since then, I'm proud of all the people working hard and smart at making our world a better place. And I keep that tipping point in mind. How can we get there? One investor at a time.

EXERCISE: LET'S DISCOVER HOW YOU WANT TO CONTRIBUTE

Determine how best you can support the causes close to your heart—through time, talent, or treasure. Over the years, I have done a mix of all three. Sometimes I find I don't have any extra money to support my causes. During those times I tend to give more time and talent.

Time: Ask yourself: "How many hours can I realistically dedicate monthly?"

Talent: In Chapter 1, you made a list of your skills. Ask yourself: "How can my specific talents benefit my chosen causes?"

Treasure: Consider your financial capacity. Even small contributions can have big impacts. Ask yourself: "How much money would I be willing to invest to help the causes I care about? Over what time period? Monthly? Annually?"

Make-a-Contribution Plan: For example, "I will work with entrepreneurs three hours a month (time), offer one bookkeeping review (talent), and invest $1,000 annually (treasure)."

Remember, every little bit counts, and the way you choose to contribute is personal to you and your capabilities, which vary at different times of the year and stages of life. Even referring customers or writing a positive review can make a big difference.

_____

_____

_____

_____

_____

_____

_____

_____

Now take your answers and fill them in the "How I want to contribute" box on your Halo Strategy™ worksheet.

Chapter Five

DISSECTING THE DISPARITY— WHY DO WOMEN GET LESS THAN 3 PERCENT?

Izzy COULD HEAR MY EYES ROLL as he explained his plans to play a third round of golf for the week. Early in our relationship, we would have "discussions" (more like arguments) about the amount of golf he played. I'm not a golfer, and I found his hobby very time consuming and interfering with plans to do other weekend activities. "Why can't golf take the same amount of time as a yoga class?" I would say to him during these talks.

During one discussion, as we were going back and forth about the time and the cost of this diversion, I found myself saying, "I'm not annoyed you are playing golf. I'm annoyed you get access to people I don't have the opportunity to get access to." I realized I was jealous. For example, only a week prior, he had played golf with the CEO of a well-known company. Golf isn't just a way to meet people and shake hands. It takes *four to five hours* to play. That is a significant amount of time to get to know someone as a little white (or in Izzy's case, yellow) ball gets hit around a big grassy area with sand—eighteen times. A round of golf can lead to deeper associations, which can result in more business deals, career opportunities, and access to investments.

I've told this story many times, from dinner with friends to keynote speeches. Sometimes people ask me why I didn't "just play golf." Unfortunately, that's not the solution. Even if I wanted to play golf, women don't have the same access to the broad network of people my husband has through golf. According to the National Golf Foundation, 77 percent of men in the US play golf, and only 22 percent of women. Maybe if I spent hours and hours practicing I could get good enough at golf to be able to hold my own on the course to play with some of the people my husband gets access to. But I would not be getting access to women in the same way, as they aren't on the golf course. My quest has been to find a "golf course" that was more in line with networking how I want to. Angel investing has given me that opportunity.

WOMEN GET LESS THAN 3 PERCENT OF VENTURE FUNDING?

Less than 3 percent? I was shocked when I first heard this statistic about how much funding goes to female entrepreneurs. Women are roughly 50 percent of the population in the US. I can't believe they only have 3 percent of the good ideas, especially since women own 40 percent of the businesses in the US. I learned about this when I joined the angel group Golden Seeds in New York City.

Let me clarify this 3 percent statistic. According to Bloomberg, women have only been able to raise around 2 or 3 percent of *venture capital* funding for many years. Even as of early 2024, we have not seen those numbers change. However, in the angel world, the numbers are better. Every year, the ACA collects data from its members to produce the Angel Funder's Report (AFR). The 2023 AFR showed that 25 percent of funding went to female entrepreneurs. So why is there still so much focus on the 3 percent number? Because the amount of money invested by venture capitalists is at least ten times as much as angels invest in a year, according to the SEC. However, the AFR data is encouraging. If, at the earliest stages of these start-ups, we can start to move the needle toward more funding going to females, then I'm hopeful we can continue to improve where we are now as well as move this upstream.

In 2013, Izzy and I left Pittsburgh and moved to the Big Apple. I had been learning so much with BlueTree Allied Angels in Pittsburgh that I wasn't sure how to find a new group now that we were moving. Earlier that year I had attended the ACA's annual summit. I felt like I had found Disneyland for angel investing! There were keynote speakers, breakout sessions, workshops, and networking dinners at the three-day summit. There were four different breakout sessions at a time, and I was so conflicted about which one to go to because they all looked so interesting. I learned about the latest trends, investment terms, and ways to evaluate companies, and I was able to meet a lot of other angels from around the world. I noticed there were not nearly as many women attendees as men. There was a line for the *men's* room. Wow. I don't know that I had seen that before.

I met a few other female angel investors at that summit, most of whom were members of a national angel group called Golden Seeds. They invest in "women-led" companies where women-led is defined as having at least one woman on the management team with significant ownership in the company.

Upon moving to New York City, I reached out to Loretta McCarthy, whom I had met at the summit. She is one of the leaders of Golden Seeds. I went to a meeting to see if I wanted to join a local angel group, even though I was still a member of BlueTree. Most angels I knew were only members of one group, usually in their hometown. I decided to join Golden Seeds and quickly realized the value I could bring by helping entrepreneurs access the investors in both groups.

Fundraising is an extremely difficult and time-consuming process for any founder. As I began hearing female founders pitch their companies at Golden Seeds, I saw how much more difficult it was for women. The amount of funding going to women is so low, at less than 3 percent annually, and women of color get less than 1 percent. This needs to change, but before we know how to change it, we must explore why.

THE HISTORY OF WOMEN'S ACCESS TO OPPORTUNITY

Before developing a plan for change, let's look at the history. Before World War II, the workforce participation rate for women was 28 percent.[4] By 2021, six decades later, the participation of women has risen to 56 percent.

The entry of women into the workforce after World War II was a catalyst for significant changes in society and the economy in the following decades. As more and more women took on paid employment outside the home, the traditional gender roles began to shift, challenging the notion that women's primary role was to be homemakers and caregivers.

The Civil Rights Act of 1964 prohibited employment discrimination based on gender, among other things, providing legal protection for women in the workplace. This opened even more opportunities for women, and many entered previously male-dominated fields such as medicine, law, and finance.

The feminist movement of the 1960s and 1970s further pushed for greater gender equality, advocating for equal pay, reproductive rights, and an end to gender-based discrimination in all areas of society. As a result, women gained greater access to education, job training, and leadership positions.

Despite these advancements, women, especially women of color, still face significant challenges with access to opportunities, people, and education. Women of color are both ostracized and discriminated against in the workplace, especially when it comes to leadership roles. Even within the context of women gaining more rights, some women still struggle, and we may never know what great ideas they have due to the unfair obstacles placed before them.

Another part of history is a term I call "generational net-working" when talking about the access men get over women in many circumstances. Historically, many networking avenues, such as golf, community clubs, and alumni groups, just to name a few, were accessible predominantly to white men. The roots of many of these relationships were built over generations. This is a broader issue affecting not just women but all minority groups. To be clear, I'm not saying men are bad or it's their fault; this is simply history, and it has become embedded in our culture.

HOW TO INCREASE THE AMOUNT OF CAPITAL TO WOMEN

Looking back at history, women have made substantial career advancements in medicine and law, but the needle hasn't moved in venture capital. The 3 percent number is one we have heard for many years. I was hoping I would see the numbers change by 2022, ten years after I started angel investing. But they have not.

How can we change this?

1. Involvement: We need more people getting involved who look like the founders. We won't change how much funding goes to underrepresented founders until we change who is involved in making the investment decisions.

2. Biases: Everyone has biases, both men and women. There needs to be more education about the biases and how we can counteract them.

3. Access: We need to create more "golf courses." More ways for different people to connect.

INVOLVEMENT: WHO WRITES THE CHECK MATTERS

Only a small minority of the check writers in venture capital are female. But should it really matter who is writing the check if there is intentionality to get more funding to women? It shouldn't matter, but it does. Here are some examples as to why.

Entrepreneur Sarah pitched her femtech (the hip name for women's health nowadays) company, working to solve female incontinence (involuntary leakage of urine) issues, to a group of male investors. After hearing she was rejected for funding, she found out they didn't want to invest in female products if it meant they had to say words related to the female anatomy in a weekly meeting while reviewing each portfolio company. Sarah heard from another group of male investors that they didn't believe their wives had these issues and that, therefore, the reported number of people with this issue must be overestimated. By the way, according to the Mayo Clinic, incontinence issues affect 50 percent of adult women. Women have a more receptive audience when the investors they are pitching to are also women.

For example, we haven't seen many advancements in female products like tampons or other menstrual materials, but I hear many ads for treatment of erectile dysfunction.

Female founders spearheading women's health products and advances struggle to get funding, mainly from male investors. However, the number of female investors is much lower than that of male investors—and therein lies the problem. According to *Harvard Business Review*, only 15 percent of checkwriters are female.

Another issue is the perception that women are not as strong at running a company as men. There have been a few studies showing the results women get. The chart on the following page shows those results.

Venture investments performance by gender

Outperformance of female-founded companies over all-male founding teams

Sources: First Round Capital

Funds invested / Revenues generated US$M

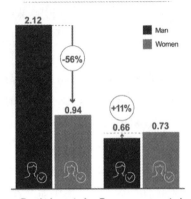

Sources: MassChallenge BCG
Note: Of the 350 companies, 258 had male founders, 92 female founders / cofounders

Graphic Credit: Mindshift Capital

- First Round Capital did a study of all their funded companies. They found that female-founded companies outperformed their male-founded companies by 63 percent.

- MassChallenge BCG studied the results of funds investing in male- vs. female-founded companies ($2.12 million for men vs $940,000 for women). Female-founded companies generated 11 percent more in revenue ($560,000 for men, $730,000 for women) than the male teams. Women got 56 percent less funding but generated 11 percent more revenue.

Due to my exposure to hundreds of start-ups, where more than 50 percent are women-led, I have had a front-row seat to women's struggles to fund and build their companies. Women tend to be scrappier, stretch money farther, and are more efficient with time than men. I'm delighted to see studies finally being done to show the results women are getting. As a female angel, I can't count how many times my male angel colleagues have sent me information about a start-up simply because the founder was female. They didn't even look at the company themselves; they just saw a female and passed it along to the "investors who help those companies." When I asked if they were interested in investing, they would admit they didn't even look at the details once they realized a woman was at the helm.

We need men to support women-led companies because the companies are good, not just because they have a female founder. There is a prevailing "bro culture," especially in tech-driven businesses and among the VCs in Silicon Valley. The intentionality comes when angels and VCs make a point to screen a minimum percentage of women-led businesses. I have seen this work with several groups. Each set a goal of ensuring their members saw a minimum number of women-led companies annually. Because of this goal, they sought out what they might have overlooked otherwise, exposing their members to new and exciting innovations.

BIASES: HOW WE ASK QUESTIONS MATTERS

Funding disparity can also be attributed to ingrained bias. Biases can be conscious or unconscious. Conscious bias means we are aware of the bias. According to a study by the United Nations related to gender bias, 90 percent of men and 84 percent of women reported some biased attitudes toward women.[5] If it is reported, it's conscious.

Unconscious bias is a little more challenging to measure. Investors tend to back entrepreneurs with similar backgrounds to themselves. The Harvard Business Review found that VCs tend to ask male entrepreneurs about growth potential, while female entrepreneurs are questioned about the likelihood of losses.

The article "Male and Female Entrepreneurs Get Asked Different Questions by VCs—and It Affects How Much Funding They Get," by Dana Kanze, Laura Huang, Mark A. Conley, and E. Tory Higgins, reveals a significant gender disparity in the VC industry. The authors found that male and female entrepreneurs tend to be asked different types of questions by venture capitalists, which subsequently affects the amount of funding they receive.

Male entrepreneurs are often asked "promotion-focused" questions, emphasizing potential gains and opportunities in their ventures. In contrast, female entrepreneurs are more likely to face "prevention-focused" questions, which focus on potential risks and losses. This discrepancy in questioning is linked to implicit gender bias and contributes to the disparity in funding between male- and female-led start-ups.

As a result, women entrepreneurs face more challenges in raising funds, limiting their business's growth and success. The authors recommend that venture capitalists reform their best practices for data intake, underscoring the need to amend pitch, due diligence, and investment-committee protocols to ensure consistency in the mix of promotion versus prevention questions regardless of candidate personal characteristics like gender.

In the meantime, women entrepreneurs are encouraged to remain determined, outspoken, and well prepared for pitch meetings. Local entrepreneur support groups can help with contract drafting, pitch-deck preparation, and financial forecasting while enabling entrepreneurs to practice responding to investor questions by incorporating promotion-focused information. The article emphasizes that supporting women in business is good for the individual entrepreneur, society, and the economy as a whole, given female-led businesses are documented to be comparable to their male-led business counterparts in terms of quality, growth, and profitability prospects.

One VC is working to take the bias out of the decision-making process. Connectic Ventures is a unique venture capital firm based in Covington, Kentucky, that takes an entirely data-driven approach when looking at investments. When I first met General Partner Kim Banham, I was fascinated to learn about Wendel, a technology platform the firm had built. This technology uses AI and machine learning to analyze the deal flow and provide valuable feedback to founders. Wendel eliminates bias by treating every company equally and asking the same questions without bias. As a result, Connectic Ventures has a portfolio of 64 percent female and minority founders, much above industry standards.

One of the unique aspects of the Wendel platform is the behavioral assessment called TeamPrint. The assessment helps the firm understand and assess the team accurately to identify leaders and give the team balance. This information is used in the investment decision-making process. Connectic Ventures looks at the personality type of each individual to see if they all complement one another. This information helps the firm provide feedback to founders, including hiring recommendations.

ACCESS: WHO WE KNOW MATTERS

Like my golf course conversation with my husband, access for founders to funders matters. Syndication, the ability for angels and angel groups to invest together, is challenging for a few reasons. Trust is the number one reason angels invest together—because they trust one another to evaluate applicants and do proper due diligence. However, it takes a long time to build that level of trust through either going to conferences together, meeting with mentoring companies, or just living in the same area. The ACA member benefits include several ways to get to know other angels. There are regional and national events as well as online peer groups.

In 2017, several of us female angels were at the annual ACA women's reception sponsored by Foley Hoag (FH), a Boston law firm. FH has been a pioneer in working to bring women together to invest for change. While talking with FH partner Meredith Haviland, we decided we needed a way to syndicate investing in women-led companies. Since I was already an ACA board member, I, along with the ACA membership director, Sarah Dickey, began holding monthly Zoom calls, and the Growing Women's Capital (GWC) group was formed. GWC is open to any ACA member interested in investing in female founders. GWC meets monthly, featuring two or three women-led companies. Each company is given about seven minutes to pitch and then has five minutes for Q&A. In the last fifteen minutes of the hour, the investors have a private discussion about the companies showcased. Several female founders have told me how valuable GWC has been to them, as it saves them time by presenting to several different groups and angels at once instead of each individually. This then led to Foley Hoag hosting an annual ACA Women's Investor Forum each fall bringing together both experienced and new female angels to share best practices and talk about the most recent trends.

FUNDING IS A STRUGGLE FOR WOMEN, BUT FOR PEOPLE OF COLOR, IT IS WORSE

My focus on helping women get more capital to fund their businesses started when I joined Golden Seeds in 2014. From my heightened awareness of women's limitations, I learned that, unfortunately, all minority business owners struggle to get funding. According to Crunchbase, Black entrepreneurs get less than 2 percent of venture funding, and Black women less than 1 percent. The reasons the funding is so low for founders of color are the same as for women: involvement, biases, and access.

Related to involvement, the number of angels who are Black is 1.3 percent. Eli Velasquez from Chapter 4 and his colleague, Samer Yousif, a venture capitalist, founded the Investors of Color network in 2020. I served as one of their early advisory board members. Eli and Samer created a robust database of all the angel investors, angel groups, and funds with investors who are Black or Latino. As they gathered information about each, they realized several groups or individuals wanted to invest in the same types of companies but didn't know one another. Investors of Color became a community for sharing the best deal flow that would otherwise not be accessible to underrepresented investors.

Related to biases, there hasn't been a specific study done similar to the one Dana Kanze did on the biases related to the wording of questions directed at women. I believe those similar biases exist for people of color and could be worse. I can share some pieces of data that tell an interesting story. For years before 2020 and the riots related to George Floyd's death, the statistic of 1 to 2 percent of funding going to entrepreneurs of color was static. However, the data collected by the ACA in 2020 showed 15 percent of funding went to founders of color who were raising money for the first time. As an ACA board member, I and others were very excited to see so much progress. However, the data collected for investments made in 2021 showed the amount of funding going back to pre-2020 levels. I could read a lot into this, but my main takeaway is awareness gets attention, which leads to action. But there has to be a way to make the action sustainable. This means we must keep talking about funding underrepresented founders and showcasing the amazing innovations and businesses they are working on. How do we do this? It takes a village. We all need to be more intentional.

Related to access, not only do people of color have fewer opportunities to pitch to angel investors and VCs than their white counterparts, but the friends-and-family rounds tend to be the most difficult to fill. The friends-and-family round is just as it sounds: it is the funding round when a start-up is just getting off the ground and needs some money to keep going. Usually, this may only be $50,000 or $100,000, and while this can be difficult even for white entrepreneurs, founders of color have told me repeatedly that this is the hardest part of getting started. It all comes down to access. They don't have the networks to tap into from people who know them and would take a chance on the innovation they are creating.

I know several angels and groups trying to solve this problem. One particular angel, Barbara Clarke, has been investing in founders of color since the early 2010s. Barbara is a trailblazer in helping these founders not just with very early funding but is also generous with her time and in sharing her vast amount of knowledge. She is a mentor and adviser to many companies and formed the Impact Seat Foundation Corporation to encourage others to follow her lead.

BRINGING AWARENESS TO THE PROBLEM

In the summer of 2023, I had the privilege of meeting Catherine Gray, the incredible producer/executive producer behind the groundbreaking film *Show Her the Money*. Having previously raised awareness for gay marriage with her documentary *I Can't Marry You*, Catherine had a proven track record of using the power of film to bring about social change. I was so captivated by her passion and determination to shed light on the stark disparity in funding that female entrepreneurs face, I became an associate producer for the film. I also encouraged a few of my other angel friends, Sue Bevan Baggott, Silvia Mah, and Rebecca Hart, to do the same.

Catherine teamed up with the talented and award-winning director Ky Dickens, also producer/executive producer. Together, they embarked on a mission to amplify the voices of female entrepreneurs and challenge the systemic barriers that hinder their access to capital. *Show Her the Money* is more than just a film; it is a movement aimed at creating a tangible shift in the funding landscape. Within a few short weeks of its debut, the film won several best documentary awards.

By shining a light on this issue, we hope to see more individuals and communities backing women-owned businesses and see significant progress to rectify the unfathomable lack of investment. The film served as a rallying cry for all those passionate about equity and economic growth.

Show Her the Money features a stellar cast of trailblazing women who have made significant contributions to the entrepreneurial world. Sharon Gless is an Emmy Award–winning actress who was part of the Cagney and Lacy show duo, who, together with Tyne Daly, were the first two female leads ever to have starring roles in a drama series. And with this film, Sharon continues to advocate for women's rights. Dawn Lafreeda started out as a waitress and hostess and went on to own eighty-seven Denny's Family Restaurants. Wendy Ryan is a successful entrepreneur and angel investor who invests independently and with the angel group, Golden Seeds. Pocket Sun started her own venture capital firm at the age of twenty-four to invest in women and underrepresented entrepreneurs. As of 2023, she and her cofounder have raised $50 million and invested in over 150 start-ups across the world, including five unicorns (valued at over $1 billion). Kelly Ann Winget is a dynamic entrepreneur, author, and business strategist. And Vicky Pasche is the cofounder of DapperBoi, an online gender-neutral, body-inclusive clothing brand. For a full list of the talented cast members, as well as the dedicated executive and associate producers, be sure to visit marciadawood.com.

ALL DECISIONS MATTER

If you are reading this and wondering, *What can I do right now to make a difference?* There are several things you can do. First, you can use the tools in this book to create your own strategy to invest and make your be-the-change plan. But there are also things you can do that don't take a plan or much time.

You may have heard the expression before, "voting with your dollars." This is something we do every day without thinking about it. We decide what companies, products, or service providers we will support by what we buy or pay for. We support certain brands every time we walk down the grocery aisle, pick a restaurant, or push the Buy Now button on Amazon. Do you know who made the product? Do you know what that company represents? Instead of eating at a restaurant you usually visit, you can look up which restaurants in your area are owned by women or people of color. You can do this with dry cleaners, hair salons, household services, and even your dentist. All our spending decisions matter.

Neighbor Jamie was looking for a dentist and wanted to support BIPOC-owned businesses in her local area. She found a directory online called Shop Black Owned. She found Build a Smile with Dr. Darren Ramsey and became his patient.

Teenager Damon wanted a new pair of sneakers, yet he was concerned that many of the goods and services we buy are made by laborers working under exploitative conditions.

Then he found Veja, an eco-friendly company making sneakers from organically farmed raw materials by people working in dignified conditions. He decided to buy his sneakers from Veja from then on.

We can take this a little further. A few years ago, I met Janine Firpo. Janine had a vision to align her values with her money. Her conviction was so strong that she wrote a book, *Activate Your Money*, which tells us ways to align our values with our dollars across all asset classes.

Janine first focused on the public markets. She didn't even know about the start-up world at that time. Now she loves angel investing. In her book, she explains all the ways her investment decisions have power. She outlines several, one of which is that where you *bank* matters. At the Self-Help Credit Union, Janine explains, as people make deposits through checking or savings accounts, loans can be given out. When a couple in Chicago was in danger of losing their home after forty years and needed to refinance their home equity line, Self-Help was able to step in and give them an affordable option when no other bank would.

There are websites such asyousow.org and investyourvalues. org that help people decide which public company or mutual fund to invest in based on gender equality, fossil-free, weapons-free and other social and environmental criteria. If you want to know more, Janine cofounded the nonprofit Invest for Better in 2021. Their members are learning together and moving their assets into investments that are building wealth and contributing to a more equitable, sustainable economy.

What are the areas in your life where you could be more intentional about the way you spend your money? Over the next month, find just one place in your local area you can support that is owned by a woman or person of color. If everyone in your community did this every month, the multiplication effect would allow businesses owned by underrepresented founders to thrive and bring more diverse options to the customers supporting them.

CREATING OUR OWN GOLF COURSE

After the conversation I had with Izzy, when I realized I was jealous of his access to people he golfs with, I actively started the search for my golf course. Angel investing has become my version of what I was looking for. I have access to meet people I would never have met before. I get a front-row seat to innovations happening in my local area as well as nationwide. But more than that, my own quest for access has heightened my awareness of other people's exclusion. I'm more intentional about finding that access for myself and helping open opportunities for others.

Chapter Six

UNPACKING YOUR TOOLBOX: ENTREPRENEURS NEED MORE THAN MONEY

CENSORED. THAT IS THE WORD COLETTE COURTION used to describe what was happening to her company. Joylux started with a product to help solve the issue of female incontinence. They now have a variety of products to help improve women's pelvic floor health and sexual function. The road to getting these very needed women's health products to market has been a rocky one. Rockier than what most entrepreneurs usually must go through.

As a female founder, Colette was already at a disadvantage due to unconscious bias, which we covered in the last chapter. Now add into the mix a topic not just about women's health but about women's sexual health. Colette has struggled to get funding for Joylux because many of the investors she pitched to, at least in the beginning, were men. She faced the same challenges as Sarah (described in the previous chapter): male investors told Colette that they didn't believe this was an actual problem women faced because their wives didn't have these problems, and they didn't want to discuss "vaginas" at their Monday morning meetings, so they would pass. Colette anticipated and was ready to handle these struggles. What she wasn't expecting was the censorship within social media and selling on the Amazon platform.

Joylux ran into issues related to their product portrayal on Facebook and Amazon, which mistakenly classified their product as pornographic. This led to their expulsion from Facebook ads and the removal of their Amazon store, which had previously generated millions of dollars in revenue. The loss of their Amazon store also meant that numerous positive product reviews vanished. Colette and her team worked frantically to try to reestablish the Amazon store and get their ads running again. Two things happened to help move this in the right direction. First, Colette was speaking at an event where, by coincidence, a lawyer for Meta was in the audience, a *female* lawyer; we'll call her Lori. During her talk, Colette explained the issues she was having with the ads, especially how the algorithms were written by men who generalize terminology, creating confusion about what is health-related, what is not, and what is just wrong. Lori was outraged. She then took it upon herself to help Joylux.

The second glimmer of hope came from an investor. Every time Colette has a new investor join the Joylux family, she makes a point to get to know them. She then can leverage the skills and strengths of her investor network when needed. Colette is also very good at keeping investors updated quarterly on everything happening within the company, both the good and the bad.

One of the investors happened to be a VP at Meta and was able to step in and help. Challenges still arise, but with the help of these two people, Colette has had an easier time navigating the censorship. Expertise of all kinds can help a start-up. And as you saw in this example, not everyone who helps a start-up needs to have invested money.

This example shows two people stepping in to help Joylux. One was an investor, and one was not. Both helped in a specific situation that didn't take much time. "Help" can come in so many different shapes and sizes. Some people work with a company on a regular basis, and others only step in when needed. If providing some needed assistance to a start-up sounds like something in your wheelhouse, you can set the pace and level—a little or a lot. Maybe once a month or once a year. The beauty is that it's up to you. And every little bit helps.

TALKING TO INVESTORS BEFORE MONEY IS NEEDED

So how do you find a company you may want to help? You can find more specifics on this in the "Where to Start" section at the end of this book, but beginning by building relationships will help both you and the founder know if there is a good fit.

A prevalent misconception is that entrepreneurs believe conversations with potential investors or advisors should begin only when they are ready to ask for funding or specific support. Founders want to show customer traction and have their business built up as much as possible before opening the curtain to reveal the beautiful thing they have created. However, this can be a serious mistake. Approaching someone for the first time to ask for money or time and expertise, with no preexisting relationship, is often why entrepreneurs fail to move forward quickly in the early days. Imagine someone you don't know asking you to spend time going through your network to find the right connection to open a door for them. Might feel awkward.

Establishing a relationship can make both parties feel more comfortable and sets the stage for more productive conversations when it's finally time to ask for funding or guidance. One of the more effective ways entrepreneurs may start to foster these relationships is to seek advice first. It could start with a coffee meeting or a conversation at a start-up event. These early conversations can feel a little like dating. The founder is trying to find the right few people to be a part of their advisory and potential investor team.

Often, founders form an advisory board early on to create structure and a cadence for the advice and assistance they are getting. Typically, four to seven people are on an advisory board, depending on the size of the company and the industry. I tend to see larger advisory boards for companies in health care or where specific experts are needed.

For example, an advisory board can be very helpful to a company making a medical device that requires a class 510(k) clearance from the Food and Drug Administration (FDA) before it can be sold to the public. This clearance is like a safety seal of approval. When a new CEO is starting a company, they need help from people who have experience with the FDA. And that is just the beginning. From there, they need to know how to commercialize the medical device. In other words, how to get this thing sold! Accomplishing these major tasks can seem daunting, but with the right advisors in place, companies will thrive. The wrong advisors or a lack of advisors can send a company into ruin.

If you are a doctor or lawyer and can bring certain skills to an advisory board, great, but remember, the variety of start-ups out there is vast. You don't need a PhD or a specific skill set to help an early-stage company.

Start-ups need all kinds of different help, especially in the early days. Bookkeeping, human-resource support, or even just being someone to talk to can be very valuable to entrepreneurs. The amount of work to get a start-up off the ground is immense. Some don't make it because they don't prioritize well, or they don't ask for the help they need. The teams that do succeed surround themselves with the right support from the beginning, even before funding is needed.

Some helpers or advisors don't ever become investors. They simply work with the start-up in exchange for a small piece of equity, usually in the form of options. Options are essentially a promise to allow someone to buy stock in the future for a set price today. Using options as opposed to shares of stock, taxes are paid only if there is a true gain (because at that point the options would be exercised). Since some start-ups don't make it, advisors shouldn't be penalized by having to pay taxes on stock until it is worth something. Bottom line: you could invest no money, just your time, and still get a payout when the company exits down the road.

POST-FUNDING HELP

Investing in a start-up is a little like a marriage. Unlike investing in the stock market, where you can be in and out of a company stock in a matter of seconds, becoming an investor in a private company or start-up is a long-term game. From the time of investment until a company exits could be years. During this time, in many cases, investors are passive, meaning they are not involved with the company other than to get a quarterly report. However, some investors get somewhat or very involved in helping the company grow.

The advisory board continues to be helpful throughout the company's growth, providing specific expertise when needed. Once the start-up takes on funding, a board of directors is typically required. The board of directors is a little different. They represent all stakeholders, including founders, the management team, employees, advisory board members with options, and investors who have committed capital (a fancy way to say they invested). The board of directors has a fiduciary responsibility to ensure that the company is making sound decisions, not running out of money, evaluating the management team's effectiveness, and regularly discussing exit strategies. A board of directors has some power over the company, whereas an advisory board simply advises.

Now you may be thinking that learning about boards can be a snoozer, but the board can absolutely make or break a company. They are *really* important. Often the management team is so close to the company and what they are doing, they can't see the forest for the trees. They are moving at lightning speed trying to get the company off the ground. The board is there to watch for the big issues that could put an end to all of it. Most of the time, the biggest issue is money: Do they have enough? Where and when will they get more? Are they hitting the milestones to keep the investors happy so the funding will keep coming?

While board members are not expected to engage in the day-to-day operations of the company, start-ups, being small entities, often require more guidance than larger companies. At times, the board may step in to assist. A fine line exists between board duties and working within the company. Sometimes board members "help" so much that they put in close to full-time hours. To me, that means the company needs to hire a new position and stop taking advantage of the generosity of the board member who isn't getting paid.

The board has an obligation to keep the interests of all parties in mind when making decisions. The terms of these responsibilities are usually outlined at the time of funding, including key decisions such as significant expenditure, hiring for crucial positions, and approving new funding. Board meetings should occur at least quarterly, as start-ups commonly fail due to running out of money. Therefore, the board needs to keep a close eye on the company's cash position. It's not uncommon for board members to have frequent calls with the CEO to discuss the cash position and spending. It's vital that the board oversee the company's spending habits. Some entrepreneurs are excellent at managing money and spend only what is necessary. Others can inappropriately use funds by overspending early, not anticipating how quickly the newly raised capital will be used. The board serves as a governance committee, ensuring that everything is as it should be and addressing issues as they arise.

Formal board meetings generally involve legal counsel, have a predetermined agenda, and are especially crucial when a vote is necessary. However, the board's main role is to ensure the company's growth, prevent the company from running out of cash, and even replace the management team if necessary.

Unfortunately, there can be instances where the CEO needs to be replaced, and that can be quite the pickle. The founder is typically the CEO and is great at whatever they have invented or developed. But they may not have the skills to lead the company or may not be able to grow the company to the level investors hope for. But who will take over? The company doesn't have the money to hire a CEO when the current one is working for undermarket wages because it is their baby. The board knows this and tries to figure out a solution, but they go round and round—a tough situation that usually involves the board members trying to help the CEO or get them an executive coach. Sometimes the results are good, and the CEO can grow the company to the place where a new CEO is affordable. Or other measures need to be taken, like a board member stepping in to run the company; I've seen that happen more than once.

CHOOSING BOARD MEMBERS WISELY

Let's look at this from the side of the entrepreneur who is seeking board members. Sometimes they will put someone on their board because they don't want to be questioned, and they will look for someone who is easy to get along with. Another mistake founders make when picking advisors or board members is not identifying their own—let's call them *opportunities* instead of weaknesses—and then finding the people who can bring those skills. Like attracts like. And founders are no exception. They tend to attract people with the same type of personality or background as themselves. This is important for you to know as you decide how you want to be of help. Look at the other people on the board of the company and see if your expertise makes sense to include. In 2015, I was asked to join a board, but when I spoke to the CEO about what he was looking for, I didn't fit the description of what was needed. I decided to instead help him find the person whose skills were a better match.

Successful entrepreneurs understand that a well-rounded internal and external team is the secret sauce. And they seek out the people who can make that kind of team. Here is an example of, let's call her Alice, setting up her advisory board when she started her company in human-resources (HR) technology. Alice has a background in HR but knows she could use guidance from others who have worked in the field longer. She asks her former boss, Cindy, to be on the advisory board along with another former colleague, Greg. Now Alice feels like she has the industry expertise needed on her advisory board, but she would additionally really like someone who has successfully grown a start-up and taken it to exit, so she asks Peter; his experience is mainly in the medical industry, but he built and sold his company for $250 million. He will likely be quite helpful.

Alice wonders who might be a good fifth person since she has heard that having an odd number can help with any disputes. She doesn't have the funds to hire yet, and she still hasn't found a cofounder. She isn't strong with financial statements, so she decides a finance person would be the perfect fit to round out the group. She finds Mike, who has been a CFO before and is willing to spend some of his time helping an entrepreneurial company. She now feels like she has the people she needs to advise the company to move forward.

Alice has done a nice job identifying her strengths and then finding the people who can fill in to help her grow the company. No one person can do everything, and certainly, no one can do everything well. Focusing on finding good advisors early can help get a company off on the right foot and set up for success. The needs of advisors and board members will evolve and change as a company grows. Staying on a board or being an adviser for too long does happen, mainly because there is too much focus on the people side and not on the business side. A good rule of thumb would be to evaluate who is an adviser to a company and who is on the board once a year. The end of the year can be a great time, as most companies are evaluating many things, such as financial results, expense cuts, hiring, and so much more.

While this chapter, along with Chapter 10, covers different types of boards, there are many nuances and complexities I didn't cover. For more information on this topic, visit my website for resource recommendations.

ONE IMPORTANT WAY TO HELP THAT NO ONE TALKS ABOUT

Any board role has a cadence or structure to it. Regular meetings and specific asks of each member are normal. However, one important component start-ups need but which isn't regularly talked about is cheerleading. Yes, cheerleading. Building a company is hard work with many ups and downs. Some need it more than others, but every start-up team can use a cheerleader who doubles as a fill-in "therapist." Not a real therapist, of course, but someone who is willing to listen, say encouraging things, dust them off when things go wrong, and get them up on their feet again.

This can be a tough job because the primary job of the cheerleader is not to fix, just cheer. However, the people mentoring are often experienced leaders, so *not* fixing is hard—especially when one of the big reasons the founders struggle is simply due to a lack of time and resources to get done what needs to be done. A pep talk can be the best thing to help at certain times to set the founder back on their path.

Founders are typically visionaries and risk takers, and they need to be able to create many of the things they dream up. Along with being a visionary come certain challenges. We need founders to have a "do whatever it takes" mentality, but reality sometimes does not match up. This is another reason why the team is so important in the start-up world. Surrounding the founder with the executors to help get the company where they want it to go is critical. Visionaries tend to be excellent salespeople. They are typically very intelligent and have the stick-to-itiveness to keep going even when things look grim. But there can be a dark side.

Some are not coachable, and they believe that whatever product or service they are putting into the world is more amazing than what anyone else can do. No one can do what they are doing. This mentality is needed to achieve greatness, but they can also alienate others in the process. One founder I know drove away all the people working with them, blaming the exodus on the staff not being smart enough or committed enough. Another self-medicated with prescription drugs, which caused such a dramatic personality change, they drove their business into the ground along with their own health.

Coachability is something angels look for in founders right from the beginning. The way an entrepreneur acts in the first meeting can show signs of how easy or not-so-easy they will be to work with. This is another place where there is a fine line. Yes, angels want coachability, but founders can't be pushovers either. I have a term I use called *drive-by advice*. Early on, especially during the fundraising process, entrepreneurs are talking to many potential advisors and investors. Some of these people the entrepreneur may never talk to again, and a lot of "advice" is flowing through the conversations.

Here is a possible scenario. Taylor met with Alex, a potential investor, to go through her pitch deck. Alex gives Taylor feedback that he doesn't like the opening three slides and tells her she should change them.

Then Taylor meets with Jordan. Jordan tells Taylor she loves the opening slides, but a few of the middle slides need to be changed.

Taylor goes on to meet with Finley. Finley says the slides look good, but the order of the slides is all wrong.

You see where this is going. Alex, Jordan, and Finley gave drive-by advice. Some may be helpful, but some may not be. If Taylor takes all this "advice," does that mean she is coachable? But not all this advice is helpful. So what is Taylor to do?

Somewhere in the middle lies the truth, as the saying goes. Taylor can take in the information, use what she thinks works for her, and disregard the rest. When angels talk about the coachability of founders, they are talking more about being coached by their board and named advisors throughout the process of building the company.

There is no exact science to advising or coaching on either side— for the founder or for the investor or advisor. Communication plays the biggest role. Simply talking through situations and challenges can help shed light on how everyone involved should react. By not giving drive-by advice and listening more than talking, you can be a great support to early companies.

Go back to the exercise in Chapter 1. Look at what skills and expertise you wrote down. After reading this chapter, do you have more to add to your list? Your toolbox of skills that can be valuable to start-ups is likely much bigger than you think. I've heard so many entrepreneurs say the reason they were so successful was because of the mentors and advisors they met along the way. Maybe you will be one of those people. Maybe your contribution will have you very involved with a company, or maybe you will be like Lori, who helped Joylux. She stepped in to solve one issue at one point in time but made a lasting difference. You can make a lasting difference too.

Chapter Seven

SURPRISING WAYS YOU CAN BRIDGE THE FUNDING GAP

EVERY YEAR WHEN THE STATISTICS COME OUT about how little funding goes to female entrepreneurs and people of color, I cringe that we are not moving the needle faster. In Chapter 5, you learned about what needs to happen to start changing this, and you can also use more creative solutions. The three ways we will cover in this chapter are not common but are quite easy to implement and, depending on your financial situation, could be preferred over the traditional methods we have been talking about throughout the book.

- Donor-Advised Funds (DAFs): Investing using philanthropic dollars.

- Individual Retirement Accounts (IRAs): Investing out of your retirement accounts.

- Revenue-Based Financing: Investing capital for a percent of ongoing gross revenues instead of a percent of ownership.

If more people knew about the surprising ways to invest in start-ups, which we are about to review, we could start to bridge the funding gap at an accelerated rate.

INVESTING WITH PHILANTHROPIC DOLLARS

"Wait—I can donate to charity and invest at the same time? How does that work?" This was my reaction when I first learned about investing through a DAF. A DAF is a personal charitable account set up to hold money or securities to donate to 501(c)3 organizations. According to Fidelity Charitable, DAFs are the fastest-growing charitable vehicle in the US due to their ease of use and their many tax advantages.[6] For example, let's say you received a bonus from your employer and want to donate a portion of it to charity. You're also not sure you will get a bonus next year, and you want to continue your giving plan. Rather than give the entire amount this year, you could open a DAF and set up grants to go to charity (or charities) over several years. The entire amount committed to the DAF is tax deductible in the current year, and while the funds are sitting in the DAF, they can grow tax free. The one caveat is the assets within the DAF can never go back to the donor.

Many people have the money within their DAF invested in stocks, bonds, or mutual funds so the funds will grow until the grants are made to the charitable organizations. However, a little-known secret is that in a self-directed DAF, the money can be invested in private companies or start-ups as well. The returns go back into the self-directed DAF, which can then be either reinvested in another start-up or donated to a charity.

This allows the donor's impact to be even greater if the start-up goes on to produce significant financial returns. This approach is also attractive for those who cannot directly invest in a start-up on their own because investing from a DAF does not require someone to meet the accredited investor requirements discussed in Chapter 4.

Custodians that specifically handle self-directed DAFs are listed on my website at marciadawood.com/dogood.

LEVERAGING DAFs TO GET MORE CAPITAL TO WOMEN

Early in her career, Alisha Griffey was an innovative entrepreneur working to improve areas she cared about, like clean energy and health care. Alisha and I got to know each other through the ACA, and in February 2023, she was a guest on the *Angel Next Door* podcast. On the show, she explained that she became an angel investor because of her frustration at the lack of funding going to women and people of color. However, she didn't want to approach investing in the typical manner, as she believed there were a lot of strong businesses that were overlooked by equity investors because they weren't chasing hypergrowth. She founded Daintree Capital, an investment firm that provides working capital loans to underrepresented founders to fund growth investments that drive near-term revenue.

Alisha initially considered the traditional route of raising a fund but realized that this approach would shift her focus away from helping early-stage companies that needed relatively small investments to fuel growth. Instead, she sought an alternative path that was less widely understood or expected. An offhand comment from one of her portfolio companies mentioning a loan from a DAF piqued her interest. This prompted six months of intensive research, leading her to discover innovative approaches within the DAF space that could creatively harness charitable capital for investing in for-profit businesses.

Alisha identified three main issues: the underfunding of women and people of color compared to other founders, the overlooking of certain business models by venture capitalists, and the disparity in women-founded companies surpassing the million-dollar revenue threshold.

Venture capitalists tend to prioritize companies seeking a ten-times return or a billion-dollar valuation within five years, often overlooking sustainable, strong businesses that do not chase mega markets or hyper growth. Alisha noticed that women-founded companies were less likely to break through the million-dollar revenue barrier. These women-led businesses offered products or services that customers valued but often struggled to gain momentum to cross into higher-revenue success where more investment options become available.

Daintree Capital targets companies with revenue ranging from $100,000 to $2 million. Since its inception in 2020, Daintree Capital has granted eighty-three loans, maintains a less than 1 percent default rate, and plans to expand further. Daintree has mainly funded companies to increase inventory quickly when demand exceeds supply. Loan sizes range from $10,000 to $75,000 and commonly span nine to twelve months. This model suits companies that can use a small amount of capital to generate a significant increase in revenue within six to twelve months.

The DAF approach may be confusing to grasp initially because it involves the understanding that donors don't necessarily get back the returns on their investments. Remember, these are funds they designate as gifts; the DAF essentially allows them to operate their own charitable foundation with no more difficulty than investing in a mutual fund. With that firmly in mind, donors can view returns on their investments as further opportunities to give. And once a donor places money into a donor-advised fund, they get a tax write-off. Although they lose direct control over the funds, they can still advise how the money is utilized and, importantly, can invest that money with all returns on that investment accruing back to the DAF, not the individual.

An investment in Daintree's Impact Fund provides funding to start-ups through loans. When that investment is made through a DAF, the principal and interest are paid back to the investor's individual DAF. From there, the investor can use that money to donate a 501(c)(3) organization of their choice or reinvest it back into the Daintree Impact Fund. The money, however, cannot be transferred back to the investor's bank account.

DAFs open new possibilities not only for nonaccredited investors but also for those who may be hesitant to invest in early-stage companies. These individuals might be more comfortable with philanthropy and can now explore investment opportunities in causes they are passionate about through their donor-advised funds.

Overall, DAFs offer an innovative solution for kickstarting risky or capital-intensive ventures that might not attract funding from traditional investors. By leveraging unallocated DAF money, it's possible to create momentum in areas that need it the most, ultimately creating a more significant social impact.

INVESTING FROM YOUR IRA

Many people choose to save for retirement with individual retirement accounts (IRAs) because of the tax advantages. In a traditional IRA, you get your tax benefits upfront—a kind of immediate gratification, if you will. Your money then grows in this sheltered environment, free from having to pay taxes until you withdraw it. Roth IRAs play the long game. You pay your taxes upfront, and your investments grow tax free. Either way, it's like planting a seed in fertile soil and watching it flourish.

Your IRA doesn't have to be just a retirement vessel. It can be a vehicle for change, a tool for transforming start-ups into game-changing enterprises. The story of Peter Thiel turning his PayPal shares into billions via a Roth IRA is more than a financial legend; it's a testament to the untapped potential sitting in retirement accounts nationwide.[7] Thiel took early shares of PayPal when they were worth a small amount of money and put them into a Roth IRA. A Roth IRA allows investments to grow tax free because taxes are paid upfront when the dollars or stock is put into the account. In Thiel's case, his shares of PayPal grew to over $5 billion. You can read more about this in the *Forbes* article from June 2021, which is also available on my website.

While investing in start-ups does have its risks and caveats, the ability to use funds from an IRA offers a compelling alternative if you are seeking impactful investments without immediate liquidity.

IRAs are usually thought of as financial instruments that contain bonds, stocks, and mutual funds. The self-directed individual retirement account (SDIRA) can have all those things and more. While most people associate IRAs with retirement savings—and rightly so—an SDIRA presents an exciting pathway for those passionate about investing in start-ups. This isn't just a traditional IRA with a twist; it's a flexible vehicle that allows you to channel funds into nontraditional investments, including private companies in their infancy. Think of it as a win-win; you get to diversify your portfolio while potentially making a significant impact on the next generation of innovative companies.

The big brokerage houses usually don't allow self-directed activity. Understanding the mechanics of investing through a SDIRA is essential for both start-ups and individual investors. The process involves two main steps, which both parties must complete to ensure a successful investment.

For start-ups looking to raise funds, the first step is to submit all necessary company information to the SDIRA custodian, a specialized entity that manages these types of investment accounts. Think of this as the due diligence phase, where you present your company's credentials to become a qualified investment option. This isn't a mere rubber stamp. It's a crucial fiduciary exercise where your custodian reviews the start-up's financial credentials, ensuring they meet all legal standards.

As an investor, your role comes into play after you've opened and funded your SDIRA account. Your next step is to inform the custodian about your investment preferences, specifying that you wish to invest in a particular start-up that has already been set up on their platform. Both parties must be in sync.

The invest-for-change potential with SDIRAs is quite large. In 1995, IRAs housed about $1.3 trillion. Fast-forward to today, and that amount has ballooned to nearly $10 trillion. That is a vast ocean of untapped resources, some of which could be channeled into groundbreaking early-stage companies.

In 2019, I assisted a start-up in navigating these waters. With a couple of straightforward forms, we successfully listed their offering on Mainstar Trust's SDIRA platform. From there, investors, me included, were able to use funds from our SDIRA accounts to propel this start-up forward. It was easier than I thought it would be since I didn't fund my new SDIRA with cash. I took an existing IRA account from Fidelity and moved it to Mainstar. My investment into the start-up was made from there. And I was also able to invest in public stocks as well.

Important note: If and when the start-up succeeds, and you cash out, that money goes right back into your IRA. If you've reached fifty-nine and a half years old, the age you can take distributions without penalty, you can enjoy the fruits of your investment right away. If not, the funds must stay in the IRA until you are eligible for distributions. In the meantime, you would be able to invest in another start-up or fund or put the gains into another asset of your choice.

But hold on; there's an asterisk here. When you turn seventy-three, you are required to take "mandatory" distributions from your IRA. However, liquidity can become a stumbling block. What if the start-up you invested in hasn't gone public or been acquired? Your investment is still tied up, complicating your distribution requirements. The remedy can be simple: diversification. Have enough liquid assets in your IRA to maneuver around these bumps in the road. For mandatory distributions, you can also move a portion of your stock from your SDIRA to another account, solving the liquidity conundrum.

The next time you think about early-stage investments, consider the role a self-directed IRA could play. With more and more SDIRA custodians appearing, this pathway is increasingly accessible for those who want to make change in the world. Go to marciadawood.com/dogood for a list of SDIRA custodians.

TAX ADVANTAGES FOR ANGELS

Even some of the most experienced angels don't know about tax advantages that both entrepreneurs and angels have under what is called the qualified small business stock (QSBS) gain exclusion. You may hear people refer to this as QSBS, or 1202 for short. Section 1202 of the IRS tax code allows shareholders to be exempt from paying capital gains taxes on QSBS stock they have held for longer than five years. "Shareholders" in this case could include founders, management teams, advisors, board members, investors—anyone who owns stock. This is a big deal.

QSBS was set up to promote long-term investment. One of the other benefits not regularly talked about is that anyone who sees a gain from owning stock in a private company is encouraged to use the gain to invest in another private company—so that the cycle of promoting innovation continues.

In 2023, the ACA began working with US Congressman David Kustoff's office to expand the tax advantages within Section 1202. Visit my website at marciadawood.com/dogood for more up-to-date information on these important and potentially lucrative tax advantages.

REVENUE-BASED FINANCING—GETTING RETURNS DIFFERENTLY

In Chapter 2, I introduced revenue-based financing (RBF). As a reminder, RBFs allow growing businesses to receive financial capital in exchange for a percentage of ongoing gross revenues. This means investors don't own a percentage of the business, but they share in the revenue the company generates. RBF can return money to investors in many cases sooner than equity investments. The model is the same as the example used in Chapter 2, which was tied to a platform that also offers equity crowdfunding. By allowing potential investors to participate with RBF, they are using "the crowd" in hopes many will come together to get these businesses the capital they need.

Angels have been using RBF in the traditional sense for a while longer. What I mean by "traditional sense" is an angel's typical minimum check size is in the thousands of dollars, not hundreds. To explain more details about RBF, I'll use information from *The Angel Next Door* podcast episode with Denise Dunlap that debuted in October 2023. Denise is the cofounder and managing partner at Sage Growth Capital alongside her partners, Kevin Learned and Molly Otter.

Sage Growth Capital became interested in revenue-based finance as a unique and innovative funding model in 2018. They decided to raise a fund for angel investors using RBF as the main way to get capital to entrepreneurs.

So, what exactly is RBF, and how does it work? At its core, it is a hybrid between a loan and an equity investment. It offers an alternative funding solution for companies that may not fit the traditional mold or that might have been overlooked by other capital sources. It was born out of the need to empower companies that possess recurring revenue streams but might not be suitable candidates for conventional loans.

Traditional banks don't like to lend money to young, small companies without a credit history or much to collateralize. Unlike bank loans, RBF sets a predefined repayment amount based on a multiple of the initial investment. For instance, if Sage Growth Capital invests $100,000 in a company, the company agrees to pay back a total of $200,000. The company makes monthly payments that are based on a percentage of the company's monthly revenues until the total amount has been repaid. Unlike a bank's fixed repayment schedule, these flexible payments better align to the company's performance, which makes Sage Growth inherently tied to the success of the company itself. This is why it is referred to as *revenue-based* finance.

Companies with recurring revenue streams are ideal candidates for RBF. For example, businesses that provide software as a service (SaaS) have found success with this funding model due to their predictable revenue patterns. However, Denise shared that Sage Growth Capital is (at the time of this writing) industry-agnostic and open to evaluating applications from various sectors, such as manufacturing, service-based businesses, and consumer products. The funds should be earmarked for initiatives that will significantly propel sales growth.

One of the key advantages of RBF is that it complements the funding life cycle of companies in that it serves as an excellent bridge between equity rounds, or before companies embark on an equity raise. RBF also offers a nondilutive funding source, allowing companies to preserve their ownership structure. This means that once the company pays off the investment,

Sage Growth Capital does not retain any equity in the company, providing greater control to the founders and their early investors.

Since its first fund began deploying capital in 2019, Sage Growth made twenty investments through September 2023, with the first and second funds totaling nine and eleven investments, respectively. These investments ranged in size from $100,000 to as much as $600,000. The average investment size hovered around $350,000, and they often opt for smaller initial investments, with the possibility of additional tranches based on the company's performance. The duration of repayment under RBF depends on the company's growth trajectory. While the terms initially span up to sixty months, the actual repayment period can vary, typically falling between thirty-six and forty-eight months. This flexibility allows for adjustments based on the company's sales performance, ensuring that the payment schedule aligns with their revenue generation capabilities.

While Sage Growth Capital had yet to witness a company complete the full sixty-month repayment term as of September 2023, early payoffs have occurred due to business successes. In comparison to equity financing, RBF offers an alternative cost structure. While it may seem expensive on the surface compared to bank debt, with Sage Growth Capital aiming for a two to three times return on investment, it pales in comparison to equity investors seeking multiples as high as ten to even one hundred times. This highlights the importance of understanding the true cost of equity and the benefits that nondilutive funding solutions can provide, allowing founders to preserve ownership longer and protect early shareholders. RBF is undoubtedly changing the financing landscape, providing new avenues of growth for companies that have traditionally been underserved.

Lessons learned from Sage Growth Capital's experience in just a few short years have been invaluable. Initially, they expected to invest mainly in Main Street businesses that didn't qualify for equity investment. However, they found that their value proposition appealed more to companies planning to raise equity funding, resulting in a shift in their investment profile. Consequently, every company they invested in either raised an equity round or was planning to do so after Sage Growth's RBF investment.

Two of the portfolio companies we discussed in the episode were Everybody Water and Naked Sports. Everybody Water is a premium water company packaging their product in a carton instead of a plastic bottle. Their mission is to support women and girls in other countries that don't have access to clean water. Naked Sports is a global lifestyle brand with innovative products in the fast-growing endurance running and outdoor markets. Their main product, a waistband for runners, allows a water bottle, keys, phone, etc., to be hooked to it, redefining how to carry personal items while running. Both companies are doing well, making their monthly payments, and have subsequently raised equity capital to continue their growth.

Denise was also surprised at how much angel investors love the RBF model. In Fund I, the first default occurred in 2022, which might have caused some investors concern. But remember the "rule" that about five out of ten companies in the angel world don't make it, on average. Denise said her fund investors took it in stride, likely assuming this is the ordinary course of affairs, as most of them are active angel investors. They are very happy to receive their quarterly distribution checks, and when she raised Fund II, 90 percent of the Fund I investors reinvested.

By leveraging recurring revenue streams, this flexible funding model ensures businesses can meet their financial needs while preserving their long-term potential. As Denise Dunlap and her team gain more experience, they continue to refine their strategies, ultimately paving the way for more companies to thrive in the ever-changing world of business.

Each of the investment-for-change vehicles we just explored brings its own unique advantages to the world of start-up investing. DAFs allow you to make an impact using philanthropic dollars, merging your desire for change with your passion for giving. IRAs, particularly self-directed ones, offer a compelling tax-advantageous option, expanding the potential reach of your retirement savings. And revenue-based financing provides a flexible middle ground, allowing you to invest capital in return for a slice of a start-up's ongoing revenues. While these methods might not yet be mainstream, their potential to bridge the funding gap and accelerate change should not be underestimated. If you're looking for fresh, creative ways to invest in the start-ups that will shape our future, these avenues deserve your serious consideration.

Chapter Eight

FROM DAUNTING TO DOABLE: HOW DECISIONS GET MADE

WHEN I STARTED INVESTING, I had a bad case of shiny-halo syndrome. I would see a company pitch, and if I liked the founder or what they were working on, I would often get overly attached. Sometimes that led to a financial investment too early or in most cases, spending more effort than I should have. I needed to slow down and follow a company through the entire process of applying for funding before making an investment decision. That is the focus of this chapter.

As a newbie, I felt a little overwhelmed, but I was reassured by the other members of the group who had vetted companies many times before. Within each group, there is a process to evaluate companies that speeds up the timing of decision-making for both the investors and the entrepreneurs.

THE ANGEL GROUP DEAL-FLOW PROCESS

Sometimes angel groups look at hundreds of companies a year before deciding to invest in a handful of them. If you think of a funnel, the widest part is the number of start-ups that apply for funding, and as they go through the evaluation process, only the ones that make it to the bottom of the funnel get funding.

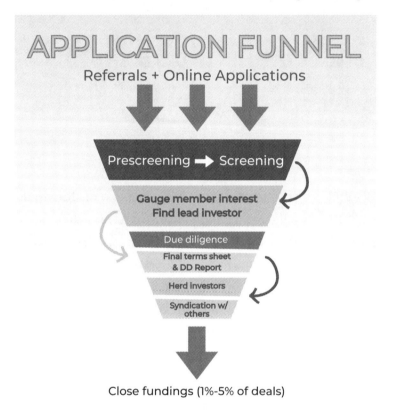

Close fundings (1%-5% of deals)

The process begins with a start-up applying to the angel group online. After 2015, software has been created to allow the prescreening process to happen through the questions asked on the application. Angel groups have criteria they want to see met before they will look at a company. Every group is slightly different, but typically included is the amount of revenue to date, the structure of the company, and the type of industry.

? SHOULD AN ANGEL SIGN LEGAL DOCUMENTS TO LOOK AT A START-UP?

Rookie entrepreneurs may ask angels to sign a nondisclosure agreement (NDA) because they believe what they are working on is so secretive they need to protect themselves from having their ideas stolen. Angels should not sign NDAs. Angel investors evaluate many investment opportunities, and signing an NDA for every company would be time consuming and impractical. They may have previously encountered similar ideas or may encounter similar ideas in the future. Angels are using their own money to invest and don't want to have any potential legal ramifications later by signing multiple agreements they would need to keep track of.

More sophisticated entrepreneurs understand that building relationships is crucial in early-stage investing, and asking investors to sign NDAs might create friction and damage the rapport needed for successful collaboration. An angel wants to see a founder who is confident in their execution of the idea, not just in the idea itself. Angel investors prefer to work with founders who are open, communicative, and collaborative.

The only time signing an NDA may make sense is if the NDA is specific to very detailed intellectual property (IP). An example would be the detailed science behind a medical device. Even in that case, only one person with expertise in that area would sign, not all angels.

WHAT TO ASK WHEN SCREENING A COMPANY

During the screening process, a few angels look through the information submitted in the application. The answers they are looking for should be found in the company's pitch. Their questions include:

- What is the problem being solved?

- What is the solution to the problem?

- Who has the problem (i.e., who is the target client base and market opportunity)?

- What is the current solution being used without this company?

- How will the product or service be marketed?

- How will the company make money?

- Who makes up the team executing the product or service?

- How much money is being looked for now? In the future?

- How will investors make a return?

- Why should angels invest?

If these questions are answered adequately, the company moves to the next phase, where all the members of the angel group take a look and investment interest is gauged. The process of figuring out who might invest is informal. Some groups raise hands if they are in a live meeting, or email/ballots can be used.

If there is a certain level of interest, then a deeper dive on the details, called due diligence, begins.

THE DUE DILIGENCE PROCESS—HOW DECISIONS GET MADE

There is a lot to evaluate during this time, with angel groups usually taking three to six months to work on due diligence for one company. A team forms, and each member of the team picks an area to work on. The main areas to evaluate are:

- The team—Who do they have and need to make this a success?

- The addressable market—Who wants what they are selling?

- The competition—Who else is doing this?

- The product—Does it work? Will people use it?

- The business model—Do or will they make money? Is this a company that can be sold down the road and investors will make money?

- The offering—How much money are they asking for, and what specifically do they plan to do with it?

- The term sheet (if they have one yet)—What are the details investors can expect to get for their money?

All this information is then gathered in a memo outlining the pros and cons of these areas. For example, maybe the company has a great founder, but the team isn't built out yet. Angels say it's best to bet on the jockey, not the horse (i.e., the founder); the team is the most important part of the deal.

I've worked on diligence teams that were very organized and some that were not. Either way, this is one of the best ways to learn about angel investing. The more experienced angels take the lead, and the newer angels help with specific assignments such as calling a customer to see if they like the product or googling for some competitors.

Once the diligence memo is finished, angels decide individually whether they will invest. You will never know everything to make the perfect decision, but you will know enough to feel confident and make a good decision for you. There are always reasons to *not* invest. These are very early companies with small teams.

As the investors in an angel group are deciding, the group leader will often talk to other angel groups to see if they are interested. This is called the syndication or deal-sharing process. Angels also tend to share due diligence memos too. Once all the investors have committed, money is wired to the company, and the deal is closed. In addition to learning through being a part of a due diligence team, angels can take classes through their angel group or at the ACA. We won't be able to cover all the details in this book, but let's look at an example of a company from application to decision.

EVALUATING DAYONE RESPONSE FROM APPLICATION TO DECISION TO EXIT

I met Tricia Compas-Markman when she came to Golden Seeds in New York to pitch her company, DayOne Response (DOR). While Tricia was a student at Cal Poly, her master's thesis was about her invention of a ten-gallon bag that could collect, treat, store, and transport water. Upon graduation, Tricia built a business around the invention. This is common. Something gets developed at a university, and then someone builds a company to commercialize it.

Tricia was able to get funding from a group called VentureWell early on to get the company started. VentureWell is a nonprofit organization that is "on a mission to cultivate a pipeline of inventors, innovators, and entrepreneurs driven to solve the world's biggest challenges."[8]

I was very interested in the water bag because it solves a big problem: access to clean water. This is a big problem globally, and we may not think this is a problem in the US, but the bag can be used in disaster areas such as floods or hurricanes when fresh water is not available, which we see happening in the US too often. Tricia began developing the idea at Cal Poly following the Southeast Asia tsunami of 2004 and Hurricane Katrina. Ideas for start-up companies that come out of a burning need are looked at favorably by angels. There are lots of companies solving problems, but if the problem isn't big enough, the likelihood of that company attaining the level of growth angels are looking for would be low. We don't want to invest in a company with a solution in *search* of a problem.

NETFLIX: AN INNOVATIVE SOLUTION TO A BIG PROBLEM

Netflix is a good example of a company built to solve a big problem.

Do you remember being frustrated with late fees, rewinding, and physical drop-off of movies from Blockbuster? I certainly do. You may also remember that the initial business model of Netflix was a DVD-by-mail service—a much more convenient alternative to physically visiting a video rental store. This business model was quite different from the streaming model Netflix is known for today. We ordered movies on the company's website, and Netflix would send DVDs straight to our door. The use of the internet for ordering and a simple pricing structure provided a level of convenience and predictability that was unique at the time.

However, from the beginning, founder Reed Hastings stated that he knew the future of Netflix would eventually be streaming movies directly to customers, but the technology to do so wasn't widely available when the company was founded.

As broadband internet access became more common, Netflix introduced a streaming service in 2007, allowing subscribers to instantly watch television shows and movies on their personal computers. The streaming service was a huge success, and, as we know, Netflix gradually phased out its DVD-by-mail service.

Netflix's journey from a DVD rental company to a leading streaming platform and ultimately to a successful production company creating its own original content demonstrates why angel investors are drawn to companies that are solving big problems. Netflix's capacity to innovate, adapt, and continuously address the changing needs and wants of its customers is a testament to its forward-thinking approach. This kind of disruption, innovation, and scalability is what angel investors often look for when deciding where to place their investments. They understand that investing in companies tackling large-scale problems, much like Netflix did with the entertainment industry, can lead to significant returns if the company successfully brings about industry change. One must bear in mind that significant industry change, which usually includes changing people's behavior, can take years to decades.

I was so interested in what Tricia was doing with DOR that I joined the due diligence team at Golden Seeds, which was responsible for evaluating the opportunity to invest. Golden Seeds was the lead investor, meaning we negotiated with Tricia to determine the "price"—the percentage of ownership in the company she was willing to sell to get the funding needed. Two of my friends and fellow angels, Kellee Joost and Deb Kemper, were leaders of the team. DOR was raising $1.5 million at a $3 million premoney valuation, which was a $4.5 million postmoney valuation. What does that mean? Simply put, the $1.5 million represented 33.3 percent of the company ownership.

$3 million (pre) + $1.5 million (the raise) = $4.5 million (post) divided by $1.5 million (raise) = 33.3 percent of the company.

This valuation was considered favorable, as angel investors typically aim to acquire 20 to 25 percent of a company when providing funding. The valuation was significantly lower than the original amount listed on the application, as was the size of the raise. The rationale behind this was to do a smaller raise at a lower valuation to fund results that would justify and support a higher valuation for future rounds of funding if they were necessary.

The target market was to sell into international non-governmental organizations (INGOs), which provide relief and aid to developing countries, as well as NGOs (same without the I) for help in the US.

The "use of proceeds" (what the funds are used for) was to hire more staff, improve the quality of the filter, and produce ten thousand water bags. These water bags had been field-tested both internationally and here in the US, so they were ready to market.

Once the due diligence team finished their analysis of the investment opportunity, we made a list of the pros and cons. Among the pros was the valuation, as mentioned above. The product had already been tested in the marketplace and was ready for a bigger launch. It addressed a significant problem, and there was a substantial market demand for it. And Tricia had established strong relationships with strategic partners such as Procter & Gamble, which added to the credibility and potential for success. The team was highly regarded and well-liked by the investors. Their dedication and capabilities inspired confidence and contributed to the positive outlook.

However, there were some challenges and concerns discovered

during the diligence process that needed to be addressed. One of the major obstacles was the lengthy sales cycle required to sell to NGOs and INGOs. The cost of the water bag was relatively high due to limitations in mass production. They had to pay more for a smaller quantity of bags until they had sufficient funds and sales to produce them in larger quantities. This cost constraint posed a challenge to the company's profitability and scalability.

Additionally, there was a lack of substantial exit data, making it hard to determine what the financial returns could be. The size of the team was relatively small, and although they were hiring, the burden was on Tricia and her cofounder Amy Cagle to do the brunt of the work—for at least the next several months. Significant competition included the Steri Pen, water purification drops, and specialized straws for water filtration. However, the most prominent competitor was bottled water in the US and chlorine tablets internationally, primarily due to established consumer behavior and ease of access.

Despite these challenges, the positive aspects outweighed the concerns. Golden Seeds helped DOR raise the sought-after $1.5 million from internal members of the group and via syndicating with other angel groups across the globe.

Golden Seeds took a board seat as part of the terms of this round; Kellee already had a board seat, so now two people represented that group on the board. Deb ended up on the board after having worked on the due diligence team.

Over the next few years, the team worked diligently to get the water bags sold in areas with the highest need. With the money raised, they hired a contractor, Yohannes Hagos, to help set up operations in East Africa and get connected to organizations outside the US. In 2017, I joined the board as an observer. This meant I would help the company and participate in meetings, but I was not a voting member of the board. Hurricane Harvey hit Houston around this time. Through our local contacts including Juliana Garaizar, we were able to get connected to the mayor of Houston, where DOR deployed one thousand water bags to families with no clean water. It was a pretty cool feeling to see all that come together.

However, behind the scenes, the company was running low on funds, and there just wasn't enough traction to get investors excited to keep funding the company. On the surface, the long sales cycle seemed to be the issue, but it was more complicated than that. INGOs and NGOs don't like to stock inventory. They just "want it when they want it." Having enough inventory of the water bags at the right place at the right time was very tricky to predict. And many times, a large quantity would be needed much more quickly than could be produced.

Investors don't like to fund "working capital," meaning what is needed in the short term. Therefore, DOR had a hard time trying to raise new funding so there could be enough inventory, and they couldn't fulfill sales orders without the inventory. It was a vicious cycle. DOR was prepositioning a stockpile of water bags at various hubs around the world. Corporate sponsors like Toyota helped after Hurricane Harvey. But the hubs never seemed to be close enough to where the bags were truly needed, and none of us anticipated how difficult it would be to sell to these organizations. While the water bag was a better solution, the easy and already known solution was "good enough" to provide for the people in need.

In 2019, the decision was made to shut down DOR by paying

off the remaining debts and closing before a bankruptcy situation occurred. While not ideal from a financial-returns perspective, a lot of good came from this over the following several years. First, many people were given access to clean water, and some of the bags are still being used today. Second, I don't believe DOR would have survived COVID, and the ending would have been much more painful. And third and most significantly, remember VentureWell, who funded Tricia at the very beginning? Well, Christina Tamer always admired Tricia's work ethic and offered her a role at the organization. She is now helping many more entrepreneurs to build companies with all the lessons she learned from DOR.

Aspire is one of the main programs Tricia now runs. Founders of very early-stage companies get paired with mentors over a six-week period, which includes virtual classes, office hours, and a two-day in-person workshop with a mock board meeting. Deb Kemper and I are mentors for the program. Start-ups never go as planned, and DOR was no different. Even though the doing well part didn't apply here, the doing good made up for it.

Earthbond was a company Deb and I worked with in June 2023 through the Aspire program. Earthbond, led by CEO Chidalu Onyenso, is working to help the small and medium-sized businesses in Nigeria, which lose $29 billion annually due to poor electricity supply. These are still early days, but Earthbond has helped businesses identify an average of over $3,000 in energy savings. And they have a waitlist of more than seven hundred companies, showing that Earthbond has a needed solution to a real problem.

DECIDING AS A GROUP OR FUND

The earlier part of this chapter walked through how decisions get made using the angel group/network model as the example. There are three ways to be a "traditional" angel investor:

1. Become a member of an angel group/network.

2. Invest through a venture fund.

3. Invest through an angel fund tied to a group/network.

Of course, people can always just go it alone, and some do, but most people don't have the large amount of money or time required to do that successfully.

The questions and overall process are the same in all three ways mentioned above, but the decision-makers vary. In a group or network, each individual makes their own decision. A venture fund has a manager or managers who decide. And an angel fund usually allows members to have some type of vote. Let's take a look at each.

ANGEL GROUP/NETWORK

Being a part of an angel group or network used to be the primary way angels invested. The words "group" and "network" are interchangeable here. According to the ACA, there are an estimated four hundred angel groups in the US. However, not all angel groups are created equal; some are much larger than others, and the average size ranges from twenty to fifty members.

Some are also more professionalized than others. A bigger group has the ability to pay for an administrative staff person or an executive director from the fees the members pay, which range from $1,000 to $3,000 annually.

Angel groups are great platforms for entrepreneurs to showcase their companies to potential investors since they can reach multiple people at one time. As decisions are made to invest, each angel will provide the money from a personal account.

Angels either invest in the company directly, meaning the money goes right to the CEO, or they can pool their money together in a special-purpose vehicle (SPV). Entrepreneurs prefer SPVs because it means dealing with only one group or entity. Often the angel group leader manages the SPVs for all the investors. The entrepreneur then only has to communicate with one person, and all other investors look to that person for updates. This arrangement makes it easier to keep up with the company and get information. However, SPVs can be cumbersome to manage as they involve taxes, and each SPV needs to distribute a tax form called a K-1 to the SPV's investors at the end of the year. Some angel groups may not have the administrative staff or the bandwidth to put together an SPV, and in such cases, angels may invest directly in a company.

The controversy surrounding SPVs is that as a company grows and needs more money, more sophisticated investors like venture capital funds become involved. These investors are likely to care about the number of owners listed in the cap table, as in many cases, a majority decision is required before anything can happen within the company. Venture capitalists (VC) don't want to have to track down individuals, so they would prefer for angels to invest through an SPV.

Here is an example. Riley (let's call him) was desperate to raise money to get his company started. He let several individual angels invest a few thousand dollars each. However, he needed $500,000, and he only had a few investors who could put in bigger checks. He got the money but ended up with seventy people as investors. Riley grew the company, and fast-forward, he was ready to raise again. But now he needed more: $5 million. Angels usually can't put together more than about $1 million, so Riley went out to talk to VCs. The VCs took a look at the ownership (cap table) and were not happy to see so many investors.

Riley spent more time raising that $5 million than he anticipated, which led the current and other small investors to have to keep writing more small checks to keep the company afloat. And during this time, the current investors were getting more and more disgruntled at the CEO and management team—all of them, now more than seventy. Riley got lucky; he found a VC that would "buy out" the current angels and "clean up" his cap table. But was that lucky for the angels? The angels got their money back with a modest return—about 1.5 times their investment, not a windfall. However, Riley went on to have quite a bit of success, and when the company was acquired a few years later, the VCs made five times their investment.

So what could have been different? If the angels had formed an SPV early on, putting all seventy of those investors under one umbrella with one point of contact, the VC would have seen that group more as a partner than a problem. The angels would have been able to stay on as investors, and since they invested for a lower purchase price per share than the VCs did later, they would have received a return of ten times their investment. Structure, from the beginning, matters.

VENTURE FUND

When I first heard the term "venture fund," I didn't know what that meant. Simply put, a venture fund is a way to pool money from several individuals or institutions, like pension funds or corporations, and there are professional managers who decide what investments the fund makes. The managers are called general partners (GPs), and the investors are called limited partners (LPs)—limited because once they invest in the fund, they have little to no say in how their money gets invested.

In Chapter 1, I talked about having a strategy or investment thesis. Often individual angels don't have one, which is why I encourage you to fill out the Be-the-Change worksheet as you read throughout this book—so that you will have one. But you will never see a venture fund without an investment thesis. That's why the LPs don't mind not having a say in the decision. The investment thesis governs the decisions the GPs make on which company to invest in.

I also didn't understand the difference between private equity and venture capital, and *How does angel investing fit into all that?* All three refer to investments made in private companies in exchange for equity, better known as ownership. However, they all represent different amounts of money being invested. Private equity are the "big guys," usually investing billions of dollars. They will take board seats and become involved with the operations of the business. Examples include Blackstone and CVC Capital.

Venture capital refers to funds sized at lower levels, from several hundred million to billions of dollars for the bigger ones, down to only a few million for the smaller ones. I was shocked to find out that a fund with $2 billion or less under management (AUM—assets under management) is considered an "emerging fund," meaning it is relatively small and the fund managers are inexperienced. Two billion dollars? That seems like a lot of money to be considered small. The fees and profit split the GPs take on these funds is why you hear about Silicon Valley venture capitalists making a lot of money.

According to Investopedia, venture capital was the top performer between the years 2010 and 2020, with annual average returns of around 15 percent. Doing conservative math with those statistics would mean a $1 billion fund would allow the GPs a carry (profit share) of $200 million on top of the 2 percent annual-management fee over a five-year period.

ANGEL FUND TIED TO A GROUP/NETWORK

Angel funds are like mini-venture capital funds. They have a general partner (GP), who manages the money, and limited partners (LP), who invest in the fund. It used to be that investors had to have at least $250,000 to invest in a venture capital fund, but now investors can invest in some venture capital funds or angel funds for as little as $25,000 or $50,000 and get the same level of diversification. A typical venture capital fund invests in ten to twenty different companies, and for angels to invest individually in that many companies would take a lot of time, work, and money.

Angels can also invest through an angel group "sidecar" fund tied to the angel network. A sidecar fund pools money from the angels and allows everyone to have a vote on how the money is invested.

TYING IT ALL TOGETHER

This chapter covered a lot of ground related to how decisions are made and how, even when you "do everything right," things don't always work out as planned. Just like we tell entrepreneurs, it is OK to fail. It's OK for investors to fail too. Losses are expected. But we learn from the losses and take those learnings to help others and strengthen the cycle. Yes, I lost money investing in DayOne Response, but I gained many new relationships with some amazing people and have gone on to take that knowledge and help many other start-ups.

EXERCISE: WHEN WILL I START?

The next box to fill out on your Halo Strategy™ worksheet is When Will I Start?

Think about what makes sense for your timing. Starting could be just googling if there is a local angel group in your area or any upcoming start-up events, or exploring a crowdfunding website. Visit marciadawood. com/dogood for more ideas.

Make a commitment that you will do something in the next week, two weeks, or a month at the latest. Write your thoughts below and add them to the "When Will I Start" box of the Halo Strategy™ worksheet.

_____

_____

_____

_____

_____

Chapter Nine

DON'T PUT ALL YOUR HALOS IN ONE BASKET–DIVERSIFY!

A MENTOR OF MINE TOLD ME A STORY early in my angel journey about the vastly different experiences had by two members of his angel group. I don't remember their names, but the lesson stuck in my mind for years. Bob and David, we can call them, joined the group at different times, and each invested in three companies, none of which were the same. One of Bob's companies did very well and was acquired by a bigger company within two years of Bob's investment. This resulted in Bob making three times the money he put in. Shortly after that, another one of Bob's companies was also acquired, and he made two times his money back. David, on the other hand, had two of his three companies go out of business within the first year.

Same angel group, same city, different times, different companies, and very different outcomes. Bob was now thinking angel investing was the best thing ever, and David quit the group and decided never to discuss or participate in angel investing again. What went wrong, and how could this have been avoided?

For Bob, it seemed everything went right, right? No. Bob got lucky. Exits tend to take on average at least five to seven years to happen, and the odds are that 50 percent of start-ups will go out of business, leaving investors feeling like David. Instead of being at the mercy of luck, there are ways to protect yourself from having too many negative outcomes.

Diversification can be the key to success, or at least mini-mizing risk, in any type of investing, and this applies to early-stage investing too. Any investment professional, from your local financial planner to Jim Cramer on CNBC, will tell you to "make sure you have a diversified portfolio." What does that mean, and how do you do that?

Diversification is not putting all your eggs in the same basket. In the case of Bob and David, they each put eggs in three baskets, but that wasn't enough. Remember the rule: out of ten, five will likely fail, four may do OK, and one may be a winner. Thirty or even fifty baskets would be better.

Back when Bob and David invested in their three companies, there were not as many options for diversification as there are today. In Chapter 2, we demystified equity crowdfunding and how you can invest for as little as $50, which is also a good way to diversify. While the principles in this chapter can apply to all types of investing, the focus will be on traditional angel investing.

In the last five years, I've seen many more angel investing funds allowing people to invest as little as $5,000. Prior to angel funds becoming more available, venture capital fund minimums averaged $250,000; only the super wealthy could participate. As we learned in the last chapter, funds can make you an investor in ten, fifteen, or even twenty-plus companies by just writing one check. Likely, Bob and David each invested somewhere between $50,000 and $75,000 total into their three companies. Today they could diversify into fifty to one hundred companies with that much money by investing in angel funds. For example, every $10,000 they invested could give them exposure to an average of ten companies. So, $50,000 would equal about fifty different companies. The fund managers would be doing all the work to make the investments, so neither Bob nor David would be overburdened with deciding about what companies to invest in. And the risk of losing all their money would drop significantly. Bob, who walked away with probably at least $100,000, might disagree with me, but his quick profits were rather exceptional. David would love this idea since even today he would likely still have a few companies making an impact in the world and could generate more returns in the future.

Let's look at how diversification works in both the public and private markets. Because public markets get more press, people are usually more familiar with them, so we can use them as a frame of reference.

DIVERSIFICATION IN THE PUBLIC MARKET

In the public stock markets, there are lots of options that help you diversify, such as mutual funds or exchange-traded funds (ETFs). Or someone could simply take whatever amount of money they want to invest, divide that by the number of companies they want in their portfolio, and then find the twenty to thirty companies to invest in. Platforms like E-Trade will now let people buy fractions of shares, so even if the price of one share is more than you would like, you can buy a piece of a share. E-Trade will also let you do an advanced search to filter for the types of companies you want to invest in, be they companies offering a quarterly dividend or companies of a certain size.

According to *Forbes*, less than 1 percent of the twenty-seven million companies in the US are public. That seems crazy since we hear much more about public companies than private ones, especially the big guys like Apple and Google. The SEC works hard to make sure there is an ample amount of transparency to investors about the financials and operations of public companies. The same information for private companies gets murky because of the cost involved in hiring accountants and attorneys to produce all the reports. If you can't sleep some night, go to any public company website, and click on the Investor Relations tab. From there you will find a copy of their annual report (10-K, as it's called). These reports are very detailed and contain a vast amount of legal information. You will be asleep in no time.

The annual report alone is usually at least one hundred pages and extremely costly. If a start-up tried to produce this type of information, they would be out of business. Early in a company's life, there are many buckets of risk that need to be addressed, not just financial. Founder coachability, the experience of the management team, product-market fit, and barriers to entry are just a few. Review Chapter 6, which outlined the process of evaluating a start-up. Diversification in the private markets becomes so important because no matter how much due diligence is done, no one can ever perfectly evaluate a company to invest in.

DIVERSIFICATION IN THE PRIVATE MARKETS

Private markets are a little like the wild, wild west, which is why the SEC puts guardrails around investing in them, the main one being the accredited investor definition we talked about in Chapter 4. Since there are so many private companies and no way for the SEC to police them all, they figure it is better to make sure the money people are investing is not the money they need to pay the rent or buy food. The SEC wants to protect the investor by highlighting the risks of investing in private companies and making people aware they could lose all their money.

Most funds use a standard set of legal documents to outline the details of what will be invested in, who manages the investments, and any fees taken to administer the fund. In this chapter, I will mainly be referring to angel funds, which simply means they are smaller in size than venture capital funds and have lower minimum-investment thresholds. The terms are often used interchangeably; there is no set-in-stone rule. Venture funds can be as low as a few million dollars in size but typically they are $100 million or more. Angel funds are usually tied to an angel group, and though I'm calling them angel funds in this book to make it easier to follow, sometimes the term "micro-VC funds" is also used. You may hear the term "private equity" used as well. Private equity (PE) refers to big firms managing billions of dollars that step in and buy companies, usually when they are struggling, and work to turn them around for a profit.

LOSSES VS. FRAUD

There is an important distinction between fraud and losses. In February 2023, a few of my ACA colleagues and I met with one of the five SEC commissioners, Commissioner Hester Peirce. The ACA does a lot of public policy work to educate our legislators about what angel investing is and how important it is to the overall economic output of our country. As one of my good angel friends, Christopher Mirabile, says, "Entrepreneurs are the engine for economic growth, and angels are the fuel for that engine."

In this meeting, we discussed with the commissioner the SEC's concerns related to fraud in any kind of private investing. A big part of the SEC's job is to protect investors. Fraud occurs when an individual deliberately establishes a company or entity with the intention of taking money from unsuspecting individuals, either by misappropriating funds or diverting them for personal gain, without any intention of using them for their intended purpose.

I've been an angel for more than ten years, and my ACA board member colleagues combined have more than one hundred years of experience with angel investing. Maybe a handful of times at most has anyone encountered legitimate fraud. Now, investing in companies at the earliest stages is risky. And there are many companies that don't make it. Most entrepreneurs are working hard to create businesses that scale and are sellable. That is the gold they are looking for, which is much bigger than the relatively small investments they are getting from angels. They have big dreams of taking their creation to the world, not of trying to rip people off. Angels should expect losses. According to the ACA, at least 50 percent of start-up companies fail. That is why we diversify. But also keep in mind, the failure of a start-up is a learning experience. Many entrepreneurs with one or more "failures" in their past can go on to build a successful company within their second or third attempt. The learnings help everyone involved, the investors included. The next innovation or company will be better for what happened. Diversification, however, will help mitigate the risks when failures happen.

? HOW MUCH SHOULD BE INVESTED TO REDUCE RISK?

Full disclosure: angel investing is risky. You could lose all your money.

The rule of thumb among all the angels I know is, *do not invest more than five to ten percent of your total net worth in alternative assets, which includes angel investing.* Angels should not only diversify their angel investments but also diversify all their investment assets, including public stocks, retirement accounts, real estate, and more. Contact a financial professional with specific questions on your own situation.

Of course, angels don't want to lose money, but no one should invest in a start-up with money they are not willing to lose. A new angel—let's call her Judy—used money from her children's college fund to invest in a start-up. Every quarter Judy would email the founder asking when her money with profits would be returned to her. Private company investments don't work like that. And her persistence in asking such a novice question ruined her relationship with the founder and reputation among other investors.

The level of risk associated with most assets has to do with liquidity and volatility. Investing in a private company does not give an investor the level of liquidity found in the public markets. Although, just to be clear, investing in the public markets can be risky too. With a publicly traded stock on the US stock market, an electronic trading platform like E-Trade allows investors to buy and sell shares of stock within seconds. For private investments, there is no electronic trading platform or even a way to trade your shares of the private company with anyone else. Once you own those shares, they are yours until there is a "liquidity event," when the company either goes out of business (becoming a write-off), gets bought by another company, or "goes public" by doing an initial public offering (IPO). You can't just pull your money out like you can in a typical brokerage account. Once the investment is made, you are in for the long haul.

WHY START-UPS GO OUT OF BUSINESS

The number one reason start-ups go out of business is because they run out of money. This sometimes happens because of an entrepreneur's inexperience in managing money, or it could be because the company didn't meet the milestones investors anticipated to be able to raise more money.

Start-ups should raise at least twelve, preferably eighteen to twenty-four, months of needed capital when they go out to investors. This is called a round of funding. The stages of rounds are as follows:

- Friends and Family: the earliest money raise

- Series Seed: the first angel or outside money

- Series A: significant milestones have been hit, attracting bigger investors

- Series B: a growth round: VCs will start to become interested

- Any Series from C onward: usually VCs only

One of my first angel investments went out of business because they ran out of money. The founder—I'll call him Derek— won a lot of prizes for being a great presenter of the opportunity to invest in his company, meaning he was a good salesperson. The company did have a cool technology, but they got short on money; instead of putting up a fight, the founder just threw in the towel and got another job. This is not typical of entrepreneurs; they will usually go down with their ship. Derek didn't even send a note to his investors explaining what happened. I had to find out from another investor. Is that fraud? No, but it's a good example of a weak management team. He lost all the investors' confidence, so he will never see funding for a start-up again.

I learned some lessons quickly from Derek. First, don't follow the crowd. Just because Derek could tell a good story didn't mean the management team could execute on the vision. Second, make sure the founder(s) have adequate "skin in the game"— meaning they have significant equity, time, and their own money invested in the company, so they will not just walk away. And communication is key. Entrepreneurs should be updating investors at least quarterly, if not monthly, with details, good and bad, of what is happening within the business. Too often I see founders reaching out to their investors only when they need money. The relationship between investors and founders is a long one, much like a marriage. There needs to be a lot of communication.

I'll admit I was a little perturbed that Derek just folded the company and never reached out to the investors to tell us what exactly happened or to even apologize. Apologies can go a long way! During my podcast episode with Dr. Brittany Barreto, she told me a very different version of what she did when she was winding down her first company. Overwhelmed with remorse for her investors' loss, she took a heartfelt step—sending them handwritten notes, accompanied by a small refund amounting to about 5 percent of their initial investment, financed from the company's remaining funds. In these notes, she expressed her deepest gratitude to the investors who believed in her dream and assured them of her intention to pay it forward in her future endeavors. I appreciated Brittany's efforts. It's a reminder that our investment goals transcend mere financial gains—we are also committed to doing good. Often, our support extends beyond just the solutions companies offer; we invest in the individuals behind these ventures, who may go on to achieve even greater feats. This underscores the importance of understanding our why in investing. While writing a check, our hope certainly lies in a financial return, yet we must also embrace the possibility of different, sometimes nonmonetary, forms of success and impact.

DIVERSIFYING WITH FUNDS

As a traditional angel, to invest directly into a company or even to invest through an angel group requires thousands of dollars; the average could be $10,000 to $25,000. In ACA's education classes, it is taught that a diversified portfolio needs to have at least ten companies in it. My personal experience has shown thirty is a better number. The more, the better. So imagine having to write thirty $25,000 checks to try to get a truly diversified portfolio. Only a fraction of a percent of the US population could even consider that. The best way I have found to get a diversified portfolio is by investing in funds.

In 2015, I was invited to invest in a pilot fund to help educate more women about angel investing and show how investing in women can provide financial returns. Several of my angel buddies were going to be managing the investments, and I wanted to explore this new-to-me way of investing. The Rising Tide Pilot Fund comprised ninety-nine (mostly) women investing $10,000 to create a $1 million fund. Nine women made up the investment committee (IC), and the other ninety, including me—called limited partners (LPs)—were either already angel investors or were interested in becoming one. The capital was deployed in ten companies (with an average check size of $100,000 per company) over the course of a year. The funds were designed not just to invest but also to educate the ninety LPs on how to become investors.

During the year, the nine IC members screened companies and held a monthly Zoom call, allowing the LPs to watch the decision-making process in real-time. The LPs loved the behind-the-curtain look and reported learning more watching the IC members interact than any other education class they had taken.

Each LP got a diversified portfolio of ten companies by investing their $10,000.

As of early 2023, three of the ten companies are out of business, five are still operating, and two had positive exits returning about 38 percent of the money back to investors so far. So at this writing, the jury is still out on the total return. However, here are some of the learnings from the pilot.

- The model of having LPs (especially women) watch the decision-making process on Zoom calls was successful. One of the LPs, Amy Nguyen-Chyung, said she was pleasantly surprised at how much she learned by watching a one-hour call each month and conducting due diligence alongside seasoned angels.

- The fund wasn't big enough to allow one of the IC members to always be in close contact with the founders we invested in. Larger check writers tend to get more regular updates (more on this in Chapter 10). One of the companies looked like it was close to an exit when the fund invested, but it didn't have proper governance on the board and quickly went out of business. Our small fund didn't have any ability to jump in to help since we weren't in the loop on what was going on in time. They had over $20 million in sales when they closed, so it's not always about money either.

- This fund made ten initial investments, leaving no money for follow-on funding, which further funds companies in the portfolio doing well. While you can never know who the winners will be, many funds have money set aside to be able to stay in the game as companies grow and are successful.

Personally, I got a lot of benefits from being a member of this unique group. I met a lot of people, both investors and entrepreneurs, whom I would not have met otherwise. I learned by watching the IC members discuss potential investments and their strategy for the fund. I didn't realize at the time just how much knowledge and experience I would gain, not only from that initial fund but also from the subsequent ventures I would become involved in as a result of participating in that pilot fund.

Next Wave Impact Fund I (NWIF), led by Alicia Robb, spun out of the Rising Tide Pilot program in 2017. The fund was set up in a similar way to the pilot, with ninety LPs and nine IC members pooling $4.2 million. For this fund, Alicia asked me to be on the investment committee. I was excited to be a part of the decision-making process. I loved the sense of collaboration with all nine members of the investment committee, all of whom were women, and many of whom had been actively contributing to gender-focused funds prior to NWIF.

Kristina Montague, leader of the Jump Fund I and II, was already backing women-led ventures in the southeastern US. As an IC member, she not only brought her extensive investing acumen to the table but also introduced us to several of the companies the fund ended up investing in.

Another IC member, Dr. Silvia Mah, founded the Stella Network in 2013, well before many others saw the gender gap in the market. Her organization expanded expertise and deal flow to the fund, enriching our collective insight into new opportunities for investment in women-led companies.

Heather Henyon, founder of Mindshift Capital (mentioned a few times prior), whom I would not have met if we hadn't served together on the investment committee, founded the first women's angel investor group in the Middle East, marking a significant milestone for gender equality in a region where it's deeply needed.

The powerhouse IC also included Wendee Wolfson, Jodi Pederson, Wingee Sin, Janine Fripo, and Sue Bevan Baggott.

Another noteworthy collaborator is Galia Gichon, one of the limited partners of NWIF, who went on to launch Tidal River Fund in Connecticut to expand the number of female angel investors in that area. Together, all these pioneering women are not only carving paths for female founders but are also facilitating the journey for the next generation of female fund managers to succeed.

Within the NWIF, we used the same education model, allowing the LPs to watch the decision-making process each month. We invested in fifteen companies over a three-year period.

As of early 2023, one company went out of business, three companies had a positive exit, returning 43 percent to investors, and there are still eleven companies operating. One of the eleven is doing particularly well. That company, Motivo, is a virtual clinical-supervision platform for behavioral-health employers. The CEO, Rachel McCrickard, raised over $10 million in a Series A in 2022. This company is truly doing good—by making an impact and helping expand the number of mental-health professionals—while they are doing well.

Here are some lessons learned from NWIF:

- This fund did keep follow-on funding for companies doing well, which allowed us to support the founders and give our LPs more exposure to the ones showing a stronger track record toward success.

- Fifteen companies allowed for more diversification.

- The education model was the same as Rising Tide Pilot, but the LPs also were allowed to work with the IC on due diligence. The feedback was positive from the LPs who got more involved, saying they liked learning by doing.

Since this was an impact fund, we needed to decide how we were going to define "impact."

When we were first forming the fund, there was a lot of discussion about this. At first, we thought we would put a detailed definition together; however, that became a difficult task. The word "impact," when related to investing, often implies limited financial returns or charity. NWIF wanted to show financial returns are possible while doing good for the world. We finally landed on "companies that help people and the planet" as our definition of "impact." Seems simple enough, but at times it got a little complicated.

A company that was making baby food out of quinoa applied for funding. That sounds healthy and like a good prospect, but it was decided that that wasn't impactful *enough*. Therefore, even though we tried to define the meaning of "impact," it was still quite subjective throughout the process.

We were also looking for a way to measure the level of impact, something that would be separate from the other milestones we would track to assess progress. We decided to use the United Nations (UN) Sustainable Development Goals (SDGs). Even as early as the pitch, we would have companies discuss which one or several of these seventeen goals they aligned with. For example, number five is gender equality, and number thirteen is climate action. For a full list of the goals, please visit the UN website at un.org.

Also a part of the Rising Tide Pilot was Portfolia, founded by Trish Costello. Portfolia creates investment funds designed mainly for women, keeping with the minimum investment concept of $10,000 as in the pilot. Using a similar model with an IC and LPs, thirteen funds investing in multiple companies and several SPVs directed into a single company have been formed as of 2023. Portfolia's goal is to empower women to use their wealth to back innovative companies and see both financial and impact returns.

Investing in a fund certainly does not take away the risk of losing money, but it does spread the risk over multiple companies, so you have a better chance at a positive financial return. Making sure the fund has experienced managers and an investment thesis you believe in are the first steps to finding a fund that is right for you. Be sure to ask to talk to some of the other LPs who have invested with the managers in the past. Find out where the managers plan to find the companies they will invest in and how they plan to help the companies grow. Remember that the fees charged by fund managers can impact your returns. Nonetheless, I subscribe to the belief that you often get what you pay for. If the fund managers can outperform what I could achieve independently, then these fees ultimately become insignificant in the broader scheme of successful investing.

LEGAL DOCS CAN LOOK VERY DAUNTING—WHAT TO DO?

Whether we are talking about funds or direct investments, any type of investment will require the signing of paperwork. Your inbox pings with an email containing a set of documents to sign, often through an electronic-signing platform. When you open up the documents, you're met with a flood of legal jargon spread across multiple pages. Feeling overwhelmed? You're not alone. The good news is that when you invest as part of an angel group, you're usually covered. These groups often have legal experts who make sure the fine print aligns with the initial term sheet and the terms that were hashed out during negotiations.

I've been down this road many times, signing off on legal documents without necessarily having my personal lawyer pore over every line. But that doesn't mean you can't or shouldn't get yours involved, especially if you're going at it solo. Just know that the goal of all those intimidating documents is to meet the main objectives that everyone agreed on. So if the legalese gets too dense, don't hesitate to reach out to your angel group or whoever introduced you to the fund or start-up for clarification. Remember, if each investor decided to bring in their personal lawyer, the whole process could turn into a logistical and financial nightmare. So trust the process, but verify when you need to. It's all part of becoming a savvy angel investor.

HOW TO DECIDE

If I could wave a magic wand, there would be hundreds, if not thousands, of early-stage company funds that people could choose to invest in. The transparency of all the funds would be equal, and the minimums to participate would be low. This would give everyone an opportunity to get started and learn and decide which funds would be best for them. However, we would need significantly more people to participate than are doing so right now. I'm not sure where the critical-mass point is, but currently, less than 1 percent of the US population invests in private funds. Imagine the changes we could see in the world if we got that number up to 10 percent or even 50 percent. All that said, the choices and level of access available to angel investors has grown exponentially since my first involvement in this exciting area, and all signals point to a further expansion of start-up opportunities.

From the earlier example with Bob and David, there are likely only a few Bobs, who happened to get lucky and make money fast, and many more Davids, who lost money and now carry a bad taste for angel investing. If they and those like them had invested through funds, their understanding of angel investing would not have been skewed by their exceptional experiences. Ideally, people would set aside money, invest in a fund, and every time there were positive returns, they would use a portion of the proceeds to invest back into the start-up world.

EXERCISE: HOW MUCH TIME/ MONEY I WILL START WITH?

The next box to fill out on your Halo Strategy™ worksheet is "How much time/money I will start with?"

Think about what makes sense with how much time or money you would like to invest. This could be over a period of time, such as, "I will invest five hours a month for the next year, and I will set aside $xxx over the next year to make at least five investments or invest in at least one fund."

Brainstorm some ideas below and then add them to the "How Much Time/Money will I Start With" box of the Halo Strategy™ worksheet.

_____

_____

_____

_____

_____

Chapter Ten

AFTER THE INK DRIES

AT THIS POINT, YOU MIGHT BE THINKING, *I was very thoughtful in deciding which company to invest in. Now what should I do? How do I keep up?* Tracking a company's progress isn't as complex as it seems. Getting to know a board member, reviewing quarterly reports, and keeping up with them on social media are all things that help you stay connected. Another thing not talked about as much is how much fun it is to watch start-ups grow. Let's break down each of these.

GET TO KNOW A BOARD MEMBER, IF YOU AREN'T ONE

We discussed how and why boards are formed in Chapter 6. While you may have experience as a board member or will become a board member to a start-up, you don't have to serve on the board to get updates about the companies you've invested in. The full list of board members and their contact information is known to all the investors. Simply reaching out to them to let them know you are interested in keeping up with the company can go a long way to ensure you stay in the loop.

As a reminder, the board of directors is different from a

group of advisors. Once a company takes on investors in a priced round, typically, a board of directors is established. As previously explained, a priced round is a clear equity exchange, involving setting a price and selling shares of stock, often referred to as series Seed A, B, C, D, etc. If the company's structure has been set up as a Delaware C corporation, which is standard, a board is required. Usually, the board starts with three members when the Seed round is raised: the CEO, another person from the company, and an investor or adviser. Sometimes you will see the potential board begin to meet informally before raising a priced round, but the term sheet and closing documents will spell out the needed structure. Once the Series A round or higher is raised, the board generally expands to five members: two representing the company, two representing the investors, and one independent member.

 ## HELPFUL TERMS

Priced Equity: Investors buy shares at a fixed price, immediately becoming partial owners of the start-up. Entrepreneurs use priced equity when they want to establish a clear company valuation and offer immediate ownership stakes to investors.

Convertible Note: Investors lend money to the start-up with the expectation that the debt will convert to equity at a future date. Entrepreneurs opt for convertible notes to quickly secure funding without having to set a valuation for their start-up immediately.

> **SAFE (Simple Agreement for Future Equity):**
> Investors make an agreement to receive equity in a future
> financing round without setting a specific price per share
> at the time of the initial investment. Entrepreneurs use
> SAFEs to streamline the fundraising process, as they are
> simpler and faster to execute than traditional equity or
> convertible notes. Investors tend not to like them because
> they have little investor structure and few protections.

In every board meeting, three critical areas need to be addressed, no matter the circumstances. Even if you are not a board member, you should know these three things to look for so you can ask the board member when you are getting updates on the company.

1. First, the board must ensure the company doesn't run out of money, as this is the most common reason start-ups fail.

2. Secondly, the board continually discusses the company's exit strategy, even in the early stages.

3. Lastly, and sometimes most tricky, the board decides whether the current management team is suitable for taking the company through growth and toward an exit.

Sometimes a board member is from one of the angel groups that invested. However, with only two or three board members per company, not every person or group can have a board seat. And as the company grows, board members don't want many people reaching out to them individually. For that reason, in larger angel groups, if a member isn't on the board, the angel group will appoint a "monitor" who keeps track of the company's progress and reports back to the group, allowing passive investors to stay informed and rest assured that someone is overseeing the company. The monitor can then keep in touch with the board members and send an email to the other investors when appropriate.

The board is critical to the success of the start-up and can literally make or break them. As an example, a make situation was with Cloverleaf, a revolutionary, team-building software company. Kirsten Moorefield, cofounder and COO, shared in her inspiring episode of *The Angel Next Door* podcast that the journey of starting and growing her company was not without its challenges. Kirsten shares her experience of picking the right board member when my friend and fellow angel, Sue Bevan Baggott, became an early mentor.

From the early stages of growing her company, Kirsten understood the importance of seeking guidance from experienced individuals who could offer insights and support beyond their own expertise. That's where Sue stepped in as a trusted mentor for Cloverleaf. Sue, with her impressive background in innovation, customer research, and marketing, not only provided valuable feedback on Cloverleaf's pitch but also became an instrumental force behind introducing the start-up to their first investors and eventually joining their board.

Sue's contribution to Cloverleaf's growth extended beyond financial backing. Her practical industry experience and deep understanding of customer needs brought vital perspectives to the company's decision-making process. This alignment with Cloverleaf's needs was crucial. On the podcast, Kirsten emphasized the potential pitfalls of appointing advisors or board members solely based on their investment status.

Together, Kirsten and Sue cultivated a strong working relationship that propelled Cloverleaf's rapid iteration process. By leveraging Sue's strategic insights and connections, they were able to overcome early hurdles and navigate the complex world of tech start-ups. Sue's mentorship and dedication to Cloverleaf's long-term goals not only brought guidance but also instilled a sense of confidence and resilience within Kirsten as they faced numerous rejections before securing their first yes. Cloverleaf's journey and Kirsten's admiration for Sue highlight the transformative impact that a supportive advisory board, and particularly a dedicated mentor, can have on a start-up's success.

By actively seeking advisors and board members who align with the company's needs and cultivating strong working relationships, founders can gain invaluable insights, foster innovation, and drive their businesses forward to new heights.

Further, investors in Cloverleaf know they can reach out to Sue if they have questions or concerns. And Sue is happy to know all the investors as well, so she can call on that network when needed to support the company.

Simply fostering communication between investors and board members can help with the growth of the company. As an investor, by letting the board know of your expertise and interest in staying informed, you are already adding to the available resources. Board members appreciate knowing of the willingness of others to assist in the company's success.

YOUR RIGHT TO INFORMATION

Information rights, as they are called in the legal docs, are critical for investors to have. Simply put, this means you have the right to get quarterly financial statements and updates on the progress of the company. Sometimes the docs will state that only "major investors" can have these rights. A major investor would be someone putting in a large sum of money. If you don't meet their definition of major, you can still ask to be included among the investors receiving information.

While quarterly updates, at a minimum, should be standard, one exemplary practice I've seen was from a CEO who sent out a monthly email. He recorded daily happenings, which were then tidied up at month-end and circulated to stakeholders. This email went to investors, friends, customers, everyone. Granted, he didn't send detailed financial documents with the email, but the progress of the company was being shared so often that people's perception of the company was very positive. Even when there was bad news to report, that was acceptable because the communication was so thorough. Regular communication also prevents investors from feeling like requests for additional funds are a surprise or coming off as opportunistic. Investors hate to be contacted only when money is needed. Imagine how you would feel not hearing anything about the progress of a company you invested in and then getting an email asking for more money. Entrepreneurs out there—don't be the person who is communicative only when you are about to raise another round.

Another practice I don't see entrepreneurs use enough, but which is very effective and helps us investors get information efficiently, is video updates. With so much of the content we ingest coming via video, I appreciate a five-to-ten-minute video letting me know what is happening with the company.

Regular company updates should not just focus on the positive aspects but should also present struggles and areas where the investors could be of assistance. Some of the best reports I've seen have had an "ask" section at the end to let people know what is needed to move past where they are now and hit more significant milestones. You should be reading these ask sections to see if you or someone in your network could help. And if you aren't getting reports that make sense, reach out to the CEO and ask for more information.

WHEN THINGS DON'T GO AS PLANNED

Every company, no matter how big or small, has its challenges as it grows. Start-ups are certainly no exception. So what can you look out for? One of the best gauges can be milestones. Before you invested, the founders would have shown you and all other investors the milestones they plan to achieve and the timeline for their achievement. Now, is this usually accurate, and does it play out as expected? Never. However, it can be a good indicator of roughly where they should be when. And if they aren't even in the ballpark of the milestones, the CEO should be communicating why.

But let's say that doesn't happen. What do you do? Reach out to the CEO! This entire chapter is about communication, and that does go both ways. As an investor, you are allowed to ask questions. Now, don't be crazy, don't become "that person" who pesters the founders so much that they can't work on the business. But if months have gone by and you haven't gotten an update, be proactive.

I remember one company in particular—I'll keep them nameless—where several investors reached out to the CEO looking for an overdue update. The CEO was very upbeat and positive about the state of the company. However, a few weeks later, all investors received an email from the company saying they were very short on cash and needed funding immediately. As a sidenote, investors do get to know one another, so don't be shy to reach out to the other investors once you are an investor in a company—I find LinkedIn is a great way to find and stay connected to others. So of course, once we all received this email of immediate need, we started calling one another to find out who knew what. Turned out no one had been getting updates from the CEO other than the occasional note that "things are going great." As investors, we weren't sure what to do. So we asked the management team for the company to get on a call with us and explain how they were in such a tight spot and why this was the first we were hearing about it. The CEO and his team were very transparent and apologized for the lack of sharing the bad and ugly parts and only sharing the good. This is not uncommon. Entrepreneurs are dreamers and doers. They want to share all that is going well and hope they can fix the bad and ugly so that investors never have to know about it until it's over. I was pretty worried at the time that the company would simply run out of money and shut down, but the investors banded together and got the funding the company needed. And the CEO promised to keep us apprised of all information no matter how bad.

A great way to keep tabs is to follow the company on social

media. If you see the founders traveling to exotic places that have nothing to do with the business, be concerned and reach out to the board members. It is very telling what you can discover by following the company, but even more so what you can find out by following the founders' personal accounts. I'm not saying entrepreneurs cannot take vacations or have time off; it is just that it all has to be in line with what is appropriate when building a start-up.

Another potential problem start-ups run into is if they have hired family members or if the founders are in a relationship (married or father/daughter, for example). I've most commonly seen this where the founders are married. While some couples can work very well together, angels worry that things can get very messy if there were ever to be a divorce. Also, of concern is if the CEO is hiring their siblings, adult children, or other relatives. Company employees may perceive nepotism and feel demotivated or hesitant to express honest feedback. Not to say angels don't invest in companies with these dynamics, but angels should and will ask a lot more questions on this topic.

MY FRUSTRATION EIGHT YEARS IN

In January 2020, before we had any idea we were about to experience a global pandemic, I looked over my angel investment portfolio. I felt like I had done all the right things—diversified, invested in several funds, and invested where I wanted to make a difference, but as I sat there thinking through the status of the companies, I wondered, *When will I be seeing some exits?* Fortunately, I wasn't seeing many of these companies going out of business, but I wasn't seeing exits either. Granted, for the first four years of being an angel, I only made a small number of investments, and I didn't discover funds until 2016. So while it looked like I was evaluating eight years' worth of investments, the majority were made in the previous four years. Regardless, I was seeing other angels have exits. Why wasn't I? I thought about putting myself on an investing diet and not making any more investments until I saw some returns.

In my frustration, I called my good friend and colleague, Christopher Mirabile. I knew he had been an angel investor longer than I had, and I knew he had seen many companies rise to success, exit, and return money to investors. As I explained how I was feeling, likely being a little overdramatic, he chuckled and said, "Remember, Marcia, this is patient capital. You will see returns. You just need to wait." I'm pretty sure I left that conversation thinking, *He wasn't very helpful*, but in fact, he was because he was right. By the end of 2020, three of the companies in my portfolio yielded significant returns, while another achieved a partial sale, resulting in a modest financial gain for me—a welcome outcome indeed! Among these four exits, the returns were impressive: one delivered an 11.7x return, another 3x, and the remaining two each 1.5x. Receiving the check that marked an 11.7x return was a pivotal moment; it strengthened my belief about the possibility of doing good while also doing well.

EASY AND FUN WAYS TO STAY INVOLVED

Being an angel investor isn't just about cutting a check and then waiting for quarterly reports to roll in. You can do much more to help your portfolio companies succeed. Sue Bevan Baggott, Cloverleaf's mentor, whom I mentioned earlier, has also been a mentor to That's So Sweet, a burgeoning bakery venture. After they landed an exclusive deal with the Cincinnati Bengals football team, Sue took to social media to showcase herself enjoying their cookies. That single act got her network interested in buying cookies for their football-themed events. Simple gestures like buying the company's products, connecting them with potential customers, or even just sharing their updates on social media can go a long way. It's also immensely satisfying to watch a company you've supported from its early stages flourish into something substantial.

The joy of watching a start-up grow and succeed is a seldom discussed but very real perk of being a mentor or an investor. Sue, for instance, finds it genuinely fun to see That's So Sweet's growth, especially since they secured that big contract with the Bengals. The sense of pride and accomplishment when a company you've backed starts to hit it big is a return on investment that's not easily quantified but deeply rewarding.

The fun isn't limited to just consumer-product companies. Sue and I were both part of the Next Wave Impact Fund's investment committee. Many people doubted that you could invest in social change through an impact fund and still make a difference. Well, the portfolio speaks for itself. Next Wave invested in fifteen companies, each making strides in areas from wastewater treatment to women's health. These businesses have grown since we put our money in, and it's not just good for the balance sheet; it's good for the soul. We are actively part of enterprises that are making a positive impact in the world, and that's the kind of success that really counts.

So whether you take an active role after investing, like a board seat or by becoming an adviser, or a more passive stance by just reading updates with maybe an occasional social post, you can easily stay involved and up to date. You can do good while doing well and have fun in the process. I know I have learned so much and take great pride in seeing the companies I've invested in succeed. You can too.

The final chapter has intentionally been left unnumbered because entrepreneurs and investors dedicate their efforts to mitigating risks that a *Chapter 11 bankruptcy* ever occur . . . and you should too!

Good luck on your journey.

Closing Thoughts

YOU AREN'T MAKING A LAST BET, YOU ARE PLANTING A SEED

IF ONE OF MY THREE STEPSONS asked me to explain who Ben Franklin was and what he did, I would have some basic knowledge. He invented electricity by almost getting electrocuted with a kite. He was a Founding Father of our country and helped draft the Declaration of Independence. Well, in all honesty, the movie *National Treasure* is probably how I know details about that. Past that, I couldn't tell them much.

That all changed when I was listening to my friend Heather Hansen's podcast, *The Elegant Warrior*, and she had author Michael Meyer on her show. I was interested in the book Michael was talking about, not only for the content but also because Michael is an English professor at the University of Pittsburgh, my alma mater. His book: *Ben Franklin's Last Bet*.

I had no idea just how many things Ben Franklin invented. He was one of our country's original entrepreneurs and likely the father of personal finance as the author of colonial America's must-read *Poor Richard's Almanack*, whose financial maxims he distilled into a volume called *The Way to Wealth*.

> **BEN FRANKLIN: THE ULTIMATE ENTREPRENEUR**
> **MICHAEL MEYER, *BENJAMIN FRANKLIN'S LAST BET*[9]**
>
> "Benjamin Franklin invented bifocals, the lightning rod, and a musical instrument called the glass armonica. (Mozart composed a piece for it.) He proved that lightning is electricity and coined the terms "electrician," "battery," "conductor," "positive/negative charge," and "electric shock." He founded Pennsylvania's first library and fire department and co-founded its first hospital and college. (All remain open.) He perfected the odometer and the rocking chair. He designed a better catheter and a more efficient stove. He drew the first American political cartoon: A sliced-up snake captioned 'Join, or Die.' He explained the northern lights and mapped the Gulf Stream. He also invented swim fins."

Ben Franklin was the kind of entrepreneur angels look for: someone taking a big problem and figuring out a solution. But he was not in it for the money or the fame. In fact, Ben Franklin believed everything he invented should be shared among everyone. Meyer informs us in his book, "While the first federal patent act was not passed until 1790, under colonial law, Franklin could have applied for the exclusive commercial use of his many inventions." But he did not. This is just one of the ways Ben Franklin believed in paying it forward. However, what many people don't know is that he was also one of the country's original angel investors. In his will, Ben Franklin left £1,000 to both the city of Boston, his birthplace, and the city of Philadelphia, where he spent much of his adult life. This money, however, was not just a gift. He attached a loan plan to the money so that young skilled workers could start businesses. The loans would then be paid back over ten years with a below-market annual interest rate of 5 percent. Franklin stipulated that this should continue for two hundred years after his death. His idea was that the interest from the loans would compound, and by the end of the two-hundred-year period, the cities would have a windfall of cash to allow them to make civic improvements.

Meyer explains, "Franklin believed that skilled workers formed the foundation of American democracy. They provided crucial services while interacting daily with people of all classes, creeds, and colors. Essentially, they kept the pulse of a community's street-level public and economic life and laid the groundwork (literally) of a healthy society." Meyer adds, "Although the term would not be coined for another two centuries, Franklin's ethical lending scheme can be seen as a forerunner of microfinance."

Franklin did not believe that charity alone could solve the world's problems. He didn't simply gift the money to improve these cities as his final wish. He envisioned that building an entrepreneurial community would ultimately make these cities and their citizens thrive. He invested in the change he wanted to see in the world, even from the grave.

You may be thinking, *How much was £1,000 worth in 1790, the year Franklin died?* Good question. Meyer gives us some insight into converting historical currency into its modern equivalent, which he explains is an inexact science. £1 = $4.44. So £1,000 = $4,440. Meyer also mentioned that $10,000, when accounted for inflation, was around $300,000 today. So, if we do a little math, £1,000 = $133,200 in today's dollars. While a lot of money, this is not a huge sum. Franklin believed a little could go a long way. As mentioned earlier in this book, a saying worth repeating: "Give someone a fish and feed them for a day; teach someone to fish, and you feed them for a lifetime." In keeping with the old adage, Franklin envisioned building an entire fishing conglomerate!

Throughout this book, we have discussed the idea of how one ripple can lead to much bigger change. Ben Franklin truly created a ripple that has turned into a wave echoing worldwide. That wave can be felt to this day throughout my home state of Pennsylvania. When I began my angel journey in Pittsburgh, I was introduced to members of the Ben Franklin Technology Partners (BFTP). The name is no coincidence. Franklin left such an impression that over two hundred years after his death, in 1983, the BFTP was formed to create "one of the most widely known and emulated state technology-based economic development programs in the nation."[10] Also noted on their website is the number of companies they have invested in over the past more than forty years: more than 4,500. The impact those companies have had on the Pennsylvania economy exceeds the addition of 148,000 jobs and $25 billion. One of those companies, you now know.

In Chapter 2, I shared a story about the company, PittMoss. When its founder, Mont Handley, originally came up with the idea of recycling newspapers to create a better growing environment for plants, among the first funding Mont received was from the Ben

Franklin Technology Partners. And that was just the beginning. BFTP are true partners with the companies they support. When Brian Scott took over PittMoss as the CEO, BFTP was there to help with additional funds. During COVID, when businesses were struggling, BFTP was willing and able to provide support. Fortunately for PittMoss, they were open and operating and told BFTP to use that money to help other companies.

Do I think you and every other reader of this book will be the next Ben Franklin? Maybe, maybe not. But even Franklin had no idea when he was tinkering with inventions or thinking up ways to support small businesses just how big an impact he would make. And that wave made it all the way to 2012, right in my backyard. You can make an impact too. You can start a ripple that could turn into a bigger wave. You can invest in change and leave a legacy for generations.

You are capable of doing this, even with a small amount of capital, given the changed rules that now allow anyone to invest in a private company for as little as $50 (Chapter 2).

And just as Martha Carlin became the change she wanted to see in the world, founding a company that could respond to her husband's diagnosis of Parkinson's disease, you can invest for change. It can be both simple and enjoyable to engage in someone else's entrepreneurial initiatives to make a meaningful impact. What's more, the feeling you get when making a positive difference in the world will make you happier than any material satisfaction from something that you can buy for yourself. You know your why (Chapter 3).

You know how hard it is to build a company and how important angels are to their success, but you also know that it is more an adventure to be experienced than a hurdle to be overcome (Chapter 4).

You know that you can use more than just money to invest (Chapter 6). And you learned about the questions to ask and how to make an informed decision (Chapter 8).

You know about diversity (Chapter 5) *and* diversification (Chapter 9), that so many have been denied access to funding and excluded from participating despite research showing that female-founded companies outperform their male-founded counterparts. In parallel fashion, diversification is the acknowledged key to minimizing risk in any type of investing, public or private.

You know the difference between an angel group and an angel fund (Chapter 9) and how they can enhance your ability to do good through your personal involvement while preserving your ability to do well financially.

You know surprising ways almost anyone can invest—that small actions are all that are needed to advance big ambitions (Chapters 2 and 7).

You know how to stay connected and have some fun (Chapter 10)!

You probably know more about angel investing than many seasoned angels do! And you have your Halo Strategy™.

What are the causes you care about? What skills do you have that could help an early-stage company? What is the change you want to effect in the world?

You answered these questions in the book exercises, but think about these questions again now, through the lens of all you know about investing in change. Do you have different answers?

On your worksheet, you have indicated some ways you can get started. Does equity crowdfunding sound appealing, or does revenue-based finance? Maybe you want to join your local angel group. Or maybe you want to attend some start-up events in your area and begin as a mentor. Regardless of what you choose, you know you can take action.

So many yearn to do good but don't feel free to do it; perhaps they feel excluded from doing so or simply do not know how. This book is your roadmap for freeing yourself from those limitations. You can refer back to it anytime. And, of course, go to marciadawood.com/dogood to find the latest trends and information.

No matter how big or how small, your impact can create ripples of change that echo worldwide, leaving you feeling proud and excited that you are doing good while doing well. It begins by planting seeds where you see the need for change and encouraging others to do the same.

ENDNOTES

1   *Bloomberg News*, "Women Only Got 2.1% of VC Capital in 2022," March 8, 2023, https://www.bloomberg.com/news/videos/2023-03-08/women-only-got-2-1-of-vc-capital-in-2022-video.

2   US Securities and Exchange Commission, Office of the Advocate for Small Business Capital Formation, *Annual Report 2022*, https://www.sec.gov/files/2022-oasb-annual-report.pdf.

3   Tim Vipond, "Angel Investor," Corporate Finance Institute, https://corporatefinanceinstitute.com/resources/economics/what-is-angel-investor/#.

4   Daron Acemoglu, David Autor, and David Lyle, National Bureau of Economic Research, *The Digest* 11, November 2002, "Women and Post-WWII Wages," https://www.nber.org/digest/nov02/women-and-post-wwii-wages. US Bureau of Labor Statistics, *BLS Reports*, April 2023, https://www.bls.gov/opub/reports/womens-databook/2022/home.htm.

5 "Gender Study Finds 90% of People Are Biased Against Women," *BBC News*, March 5, 2020, https://www.bbc.com/news/world-51751915#.

6 Fidelity Charitable, "What Is a Donor-Advised Fund (DAF)?" https://www.fidelitycharitable.org/guidance/philanthropy/what-is-a-donor-advised-fund.html#:~:text=You%20want%20your%20charitable%20donations,ways%20to%20give%20to%20charity.

7 Sarah Hansen, "Peter Thiel Has Accumulated $5 Billion in a Tax Free Roth IRA Designed to Help the Middle Class Save for Retirement, According to New Report," *Forbes*, June 24, 2021, https://www.forbes.com/sites/sarahhansen/2021/06/24/peter-thiel-has-accumulated-5-billion-in-a-tax-free-roth-ira-designed-to-help-the-middle-class-save-for-retirement-according-to-new-report/?sh=468a352a2627.

8 VentureWell, "Our Mission," https://venturewell.org/.

9 Michael Meyer, *Benjamin Franklin's Last Bet: The Favorite Founder's Diverse Death, Enduring Afterlife, and Blueprint for American Prosperity* (Boston: Mariner Books, 2022). Reprinted with permission.

10 Ben Franklin Technology Partners. Accessed 1/2/2024 from benfranklin.org/about.

GLOSSARY

Several of these terms were not used in this book, but I've included them in case you need them as you venture into angel world.

- **Accredited Investor:** A definition set in place by the US Securities and Exchange Commission as of 2023 is based mainly on income and wealth levels. The investor must make an annual income of $200,000 if single ($300,000 with a spouse) or have $1 million in net worth, excluding the primary home.

- **Angel Group:** A formal or informal organization of individuals who come together to evaluate start-up investment opportunities in order to make angel investments.

- **Angel Investor:** An individual who provides support (money, time, or expertise) to start-ups or entrepreneurs, often in exchange for convertible debt or ownership equity.

- **B2B (Business-to-Business):** Refers to businesses primarily selling products or services to other businesses rather than directly to consumers.

- **Bootstrapping:** Building a company from the ground up with nothing but personal savings and the cash coming in from the first sales.

- **Burn Rate:** The rate at which a company is spending its capital before generating positive cash flow from operations.

- **Business Angel:** A term used primarily in Europe for an angel investor.

- **Cap Table:** Stands for capitalization table, which is simply a list of all the investors and the percentage of the company they own.

- **Convertible Note:** A short-term debt that converts into equity, usually in conjunction with a future financing round.

- **DTC (Direct-to-Consumer):** Describes companies that sell products or services directly to consumers, bypassing traditional retail channels.

- **Due Diligence:** The comprehensive assessment of a business, typically conducted by investors before making a funding decision.

- **Elevator Pitch:** A brief, persuasive speech used to spark interest in what a start-up is doing.

- **Equity Financing:** The act of raising capital by selling shares of a company—also called a priced round.

- **Exit (Business Exit):** The strategy or event through which an investor realizes a return on their investment.

- **Exit Strategy:** A planned approach to liquidating an investor's stake in a company.

- **Freedom to Operate:** This term refers to the ability of a company to develop, manufacture, and sell a product or service without infringing on the intellectual property rights of others. It typically involves conducting a thorough analysis of existing patents and other IP rights to ensure that a new product or technology doesn't violate any existing protections. This is especially important for start-ups in technology and scientific sectors.

- **Friends and Family Round:** The very first money raised by a new company.

- **General Partner (GP):** The manager of an angel or venture capital fund who makes investment decisions.

- **Initial Public Offering (IPO):** The process of offering shares of a private corporation to the public in a new stock issuance.

- **Lead Investor:** The first, and typically largest, investor in a funding round.

- **Limited Partner (LP):** The investor in an angel or venture capital fund who has no decision-making rights.

- **Liquidity Event:** An occurrence that allows initial investors in a company to cash out some or all of their equity.

- **Major Investor:** An investor putting a certain amount of money into a company, which entitles them to specific information.

- **Non-Dilutive Funding:** Financing that does not require a company to give up equity.

- **Pitch:** Another term for the presentation of the investment opportunity by an entrepreneur.

- **Postmoney Valuation:** The estimated value of a company after outside financing and/or capital injections are added.

- **Premoney Valuation:** The valuation of a company prior to an investment or funding.

- **Pro-Rata Rights:** The right of an investor to participate in future funding rounds to maintain their percentage ownership.

- **Simple Agreement for Future Equity (SAFE):** An agreement to receive equity in a future financing round without setting a specific price per share at the time of the initial investment.

- **Seed Funding:** An initial investment to start a business, covering the initial operating expenses of a new venture.

- **Sidecar Fund:** An investment vehicle used alongside a primary investment fund, allowing investors to participate in specific opportunities.

- **Special-Purpose Vehicle (SPV):** A group of investors who come together to invest in a single project or company, pooling their resources and expertise.

- **Term Sheet:** A nonbinding agreement outlining the basic terms and conditions under which an investment will be made.

- **Unicorn:** The name used for a start-up company that is valued at over $1 billion.

- **Valuation:** The process of determining the present worth of a company or asset.

- **Vesting:** The process through which an employee or investor earns the right to receive full ownership of certain assets or stock options over time. In the context of start-ups and angel investing, vesting often applies to the equity or stock options granted to founders, employees, and sometimes investors. The purpose of a vesting schedule is to incentivize longevity and commitment; it ensures that these stakeholders remain engaged and contribute to the company's growth over a period before they can claim full ownership of their equity portion. Typically, this involves a "cliff" period (often one year) before any shares are vested, followed by a gradual vesting period (commonly four years), after which the individual earns the right to their full share.

GET STARTED

REGARDLESS OF WHERE YOU ARE ON YOUR JOURNEY to do good while doing well, the number of ways to participate are vast, with changes happening every day.

Visit marciadawood.com/dogood for current suggestions on how to look for innovative opportunities in your backyard or around the world. Now you are at the point of developing an action plan. This is the last section of your Halo Strategy™ worksheet. You have several ideas from throughout the book, and the Getting Started webpage will help as well. Whatever you decide, just get started. It is the best way to learn and make a difference at the same time.

ACKNOWLEDGMENTS

In 2011, Izzy and I almost moved to London. I was working full-time in a corporate career, and suddenly, I was dreaming of a new life in another country. We didn't end up in London, but my dream of a different life continued. Around the time I was invited to my first angel investing meeting, which you read about in this book, I decided to get an MBA at UNC Chapel Hill. I would have never been able to pursue what I really wanted if Izzy hadn't been not only supportive but also my biggest cheerleader. He helped me see potential in myself and in what I was doing even before I could. This book could not have been written if I hadn't had all the experiences outlined in the previous pages. For his support and love, I am forever grateful.

My parents were, of course, my first cheerleaders. They always told me I could do and be anything I put my mind to. I wish my mom were still with us; I would love to share this book with her. A few years after her death, my dad remarried, and I'm grateful he found happiness again, proving no matter how bad things get, there can be light. I know my mom is looking down on us and smiling.

I wouldn't know as much as I do today if I hadn't had such

a great role model in Catherine Mott. Thank you for not just guiding me, but for all the people you have influenced to help make change in the world.

Through angel investing, I was lucky enough to meet people who have become good friends, especially my Next Wave crew. Special thank you to Sue Bevan Baggott who helped tremendously with my TEDx speech as well as this book. Sue also introduced me to the Recognized Expert Group (REx) led by Dorie Clark, and Heroic Public Speaking, led by Michael and Amy Port. At Heroic, I learned how to write and deliver a speech, and it is also where I met AJ Harper. Big thanks to AJ and Laura Stone for the wisdom, guidance, and encouragement—and for building the amazing Top Three Book (T3) community. I'm sure I could have written *a* book, but I couldn't have written *this* book without AJ. Anyone thinking of writing a book needs a copy of her book, *Write a Must-Read*, and should check out all her online offerings.

In this book, you heard me talk about angel investing being my "golf course." REx, Heroic, and T3 are the other places where I've met many incredible humans out to make the world a better place. The *Show Her the Money* family is another group that fits this category. Thank you, Catherine Gray, for your visionary use of media to highlight and raise awareness about significant issues confronting our world.

I'd also like to thank all the people who read this book early and gave feedback: Beth May—copy editor extraordinaire!, Pat Gouhin, Nancy Hayes, Dyana Pari Holzworth, Mindy Posoff, Robin Lattanzi, Dr. Kim Bowman, Marla Weston, Antoine Levy, Jules Apollo, Elaine Bolle, Cynthia Beiler, Dawn Batts, Anne Maghus, Mara Yale, and of course Sue Bevan Baggott, whom I made read it several times.

Thank you to Amplify Publishing Group's CEO and Publisher Naren Aryal, Director of Production Jenna Scafuri, and the amazing Amplify team.

Thank you to the people whose stories were a big part of this book–Martha Carlin, Eli Velasquez, Brian Scott, Tricia Compas-Markman, Alicia Robb, and Heather Henyon.

AUTHOR'S NOTE

Throughout this book, I have tried to explain my views on getting the innovation and solutions in the world that we really want to see. The things that will make a big difference in our futures but, more importantly, in the futures of our children and beyond. Frankly, I got tired of seeing energetic companies working on life-changing issues not go anywhere because there simply wasn't enough financial support and human expertise surrounding them.

All content in this book is informational and not intended to serve as legal, tax, accounting, or investing advice. At the time of this writing, I serve on the SEC Small Business Capital Formation Advisory Committee; however, my views are my own and not the views of the SEC or my fellow committee colleagues.

Readers should consult their own tax, investing, legal, or accounting advisors before making important financial decisions. All warranties, including accuracy, completeness, and suitability for specific purposes, are disclaimed.

Throughout this book, you'll find data or research I've referenced. In most instances, sources are directly mentioned within the text. Whenever I believed the research might pique your interest for a deeper dive, I included a link as an endnote.

I've done my best to show you my journey and many of the mistakes I've made. My hope now is you will act. If everyone invested just a little bit of time, money, or expertise, imagine the change we would see in the world—a change that could even save the life of someone you love.

LET'S START A CONVERSATION

Reach out to ask questions or discuss ways I can help you.

marciadawood.com

🔲 /marciadawood

📘 @marcia.dawood

📷 @marciadawood

If you have found value in the content of this book, please take a minute to share your thoughts in a review on any retailer or social media platform. Be sure to tag me. I'm looking forward to hearing from you!

ABOUT THE AUTHOR

Marcia Dawood is an early-stage investor who serves on the Securities and Exchange Commission's (SEC's) Small Business Capital Formation Advisory Committee, a venture partner with Mindshift Capital, and a member of Golden Seeds. She is the chair emeritus of the Angel Capital Association (ACA), a global professional society for angel investors. Marcia is an associate producer on the award-winning documentary film *Show Her the Money.* A TEDx speaker and the host of *The Angel Next Door* podcast, Marcia walks the talk and holds investments in over fifty early-stage companies and funds. She is committed to expanding support for diverse companies that overcome the world's biggest problems and accelerate positive change.

Marcia received an MBA from the University of North Carolina Kenan-Flagler Business School. She currently lives in North Carolina with her husband, Izzy, and she feels lucky to be the stepmom to three amazing sons.